101
Ways to Say
Merry Christmas
for Less Than
$25

101
Ways to Say
Merry Christmas
for Less Than
$25

JOHN MALONE
AND PAUL BALDWIN

WILLIAM MORROW AND COMPANY, INC.
New York

It is the policy of William Morrow and Company, Inc., and its imprints and affiliates, recognizing the importance of preserving what has been written, to print the books we publish on acid-free paper, and we exert our best efforts to that end.

Library of Congress Cataloging-in-Publication Data

Malone, John Williams.
  101 ways to say Merry Christmas for less than $25 / by John Malone and Paul Baldwin.
      p.   cm.
    ISBN 0-688-11361-3
    1. Christmas—United States.   2. Christmas decorations—United States.   3. Gifts—United States.   4. United States—Social life and customs.   I. Baldwin, Paul.   II. Title.   III. Title: One hundred one ways to say Merry Christmas for less than $25.   IV. Title: One hundred and one ways to say Merry Christmas for less than $25.
GT4986.A1M35   1992
394.2'68282—dc20   92–7447
                                                                CIP

Printed in the United States of America

First Edition

1 2 3 4 5 6 7 8 9 10

BOOK DESIGN BY JAYE ZIMET

Contents

5

Contents

CONTENTS

CONTENTS

Introduction

101 *Ways to Say Merry Christmas for Less Than $25* is intended to help you find affordable presents for everyone on your Christmas list. But it's not just a matter of saving on the budget—we hope that the suggestions in this book will also make it easier for you to find imaginative gifts that the recipients will be very happy to get. Unusual, pretty, useful, or fun gifts do not have to be expensive; terrific choices are available in great numbers in stores and by mail. But in the hectic Christmas shopping season, it is often difficult to pick out just the right present at an excellent price. This book should make it much easier to do that.

We went through more than four hundred mail-order catalogs in preparing this book. Many splendid catalogs are not included here, however, because the bulk of their offerings were considerably above the $25 level. Although catalogs often change a number of the items they offer from season to season and year to year, we have described many possible gifts in detail, and given specific current prices, in order to give you the clearest possible sense of the particular kinds of merchandise you are likely to get from a given source. Just keep in mind that prices and availability may be subject to change. A list of all the catalogs mentioned in each chapter is included at the end of the book, including both addresses and 800 numbers.

We have tried to make this book as practical and useful as possible, but we also hope that it will stimulate your imagination, and that you will simply have a lot of fun with it.

9

1
Treasured Ornaments, All Year in a Box

THE NOVELIST FAITH Baldwin once wrote about her own personal joy in the traditions of Christmas: "About December twenty-first the tree things are brought down from the attic. This has happened so often in this and other houses you'd think they could spill from the cartons and boxes and climb down the ladder by themselves. It's an interesting fancy—the birds flying, some with only one wing; the round colored globes bouncing (but not breaking); and all the tree angels marching— or winging—in pairs."

Christmas ornaments are treasures, to be uncovered each year with anticipation, especially those special ornaments that go back to one's childhood, or those with unusual shapes— the bunch of grapes, the gleaming green pickle, or the gold sequin dinosaur. Unusual ornaments also make wonderful Christmas presents. There has been a recent revival of the manufacture of mouth-blown glass ornaments, many of them based on molds from a century or more ago. Some can be found in stores that specialize in Christmas decorations, and others are available in department stores. But the most unusual and beautiful ones we have come across are offered in the mail-order catalogs of major American museums.

One of the most interesting and varied collections offered is that of Delaware's famous Winterthur Museum. There we find shimmering purple-necked peacocks with spun-glass golden tails at $16 a pair. A set of three fanciful Victorian-style blown glass treats representing a flowered purse, a bird cage, and a flower basket is the same price. A pair of particularly nice pickle ornaments—often placed on the tree last in Europe to bring good luck—is only $12.50. A set of three musical instrument ornaments, in gold, red, and green, is very enticing, but perhaps most fun is a pair of crescent moon faces in gold and silver with red-tinged cheeks and lips. The musical instruments are three for $15.00, the moons, $12.50 a pair.

The Smithsonian Institution is also very strong on Christmas tree ornaments, although several of its sets exceed our $25 limit by a few dollars. But they also offer a number of eminently affordable beauties. A set of six all-different silver, green, and red teddy bear glass rascals at only $18 would surely delight a family with young children. Four "Tiffany" shade ornaments at $20 are unusual and sophisticated. The Smithsonian also has smashing polyresin carousel ornaments, adapted from the National Museum of American History's splendid collection of actual carousel animals at $12.50 each. Or you could opt for a set of three bright wooden nutcracker soldiers with pull-toy mechanisms for only $12.

The variety of offerings from The Metropolitan Museum of Art, New York, The Art Institute of Chicago, Boston's Museum of Fine Arts, and New York's Museum of Modern Art are less extensive in the Christmas ornament area, but each has some special dazzlers that are very affordable and certain to bring on the *oohs* and *aahs*. And any of these glittering little treasures will bring renewed pleasure year after year at Christmastime.

2
A House Made of Gingerbread

"BAKING GINGERBREAD PERFUMES a house like nothing else. It is good eaten warm or cool, iced or plain. And it improves with age, should you be lucky enough or restrained enough to keep it around for any length of time." So writes novelist Laurie Colwin, pinpointing one aspect of why it is such a pleasure to make a gingerbread house as a Christmas gift.

One or more of the women's magazines has a recipe and instructions for making a gingerbread house every year. For those who find it difficult or tedious to follow instructions that involve cutting out patterns in aluminum foil or wax paper, here is an alternative. Williams-Sonoma, the California-headquartered cookware and gourmet company, offers a cast-iron gingerbread house mold with a stick-resistant surface for $20. Our suggestion is to buy the mold, make a gingerbread house—which involves filling and baking the mold twice—and then present both the house and the mold as a single present.

Whether you take this route or make a gingerbread house from a magazine or Christmas craft book, here's an extra tip from three women we know in Long Island City, New York, who get together to make a gingerbread house every year: To really dress things up, buy a box of ice cream sugar cones, turn them upside down, and use green and red frosting to transform them into Christmas trees.

3
What's in a Mug?

WHAT CAN YOU get that makes *Star Trek*'s Captain Kirk, Mr. Spock, and Dr. McCoy disappear from the transporter room of the *Enterprise* when you use it? Or causes the words *I Love You* to appear where seconds before there was only a jumble of letters? Coffee mugs, of course. With these and others of the sort, the pouring of hot tea, coffee, or cocoa changes the picture on the mug, which reinstates itself as the liquid cools down or the mug is emptied. There is something about this process that can bring a little smile to the face of even the grouchiest early riser. There's a disappearing Cheshire cat, too, speaking of smiles.

Mugs are everywhere these days, featured in dozens of catalogs, and stores. The "disappearing ink" mugs are a lot of fun, but there are also many extremely attractive mugs where the picture stays put: There are mugs featuring the planets of the solar system; endangered and unendangered species of animals; mugs with European coats of arms; mugs reproducing paintings by Dali, Van Gogh, Rousseau, and Magritte. There are more elaborate mugs, designed so that the head of a flamingo or peacock forms the handle, and the body wraps around the rest of it.

All of these are either so much fun or so attractive that they can be considered a possible present for almost anyone, giving a little thought to each individual's interests. With prices ranging from $7 to $12 for some individual mugs, and $14 to $20 for pairs of others, they are certainly affordable. You don't even have to worry about duplication—two zebras in the cupboard can be even better than one, although new designs are being introduced so regularly that you're more likely to hit on a new model.

14

Not only are mugs a good present for someone you know well enough to match the design to a particular passion (like *Star Trek* or birds), the more generic ones are a good choice for that person on your gift list whom you really don't know very well. And last, consider keeping a couple of extra mugs on hand for reciprocating that unexpected gift to you. While mugs are widely available in department and gift stores, two of the best mail-order sources are Signals and What On Earth.

4

Christmas Welcome Mats

THE CHRISTMAS HOLIDAYS always involve a lot of comings and goings, both within a family and because of friends dropping off gifts or stopping by for some Christmas cheer. In most parts of the country, that is going to mean a lot of wet feet trooping in from winter weather. An exterior doormat or small rug with Christmas themes for just inside the door can not only add to the welcome but be very practical as well. After the holidays, the doormat can be stored for use the next year.

A Christmas doormat is something that can easily be picked up in a local store, but there are some attractive and amusing ones available by mail order. Miles Kimball offers a doormat that would particularly appeal to cat lovers, depicting a calico cat wearing a holly wreath and sitting in a bedecked holiday window ($8.98). Casual Living carries a green mat with HO, HO, HO! written large on it ($10.95). A mat from Harriet Carter takes that idea a step further: a green mat emblazoned with a jolly red-suited Santa; when a visitor sets foot on it, the mat calls out, "Ho, Ho, Ho, Merry Christmas" ($19.98), batteries not included. The handsomest example we saw was what the Gardener's Eden catalog calls a Mud Rug. Machine-washable in cold water, the fringed rug is jacquard woven in a reversible pattern of red and green Christmas trees ($16.00). Now there's a good idea—one side gets dirty, just turn it over.

5
Hung by the Fireplace with Care

BOTH THE AUTHORS of this book were given handmade Christmas stockings as children, as were the various siblings in our two families. For each of us, the stocking was a present from a close friend of our parents. They were made of felt, one red and white, the other red and green. One had small bells at the heel and toe, with the name John simply stitched in red on the white turned-over flap at the top, which also had bells attached to it. On the other stocking, the name Paul was much more elaborately stitched in a glittering gold. That they are remembered so well shows how much they were treasured.

Women's magazines and crafts books are full of designs for Christmas stockings, but the form is so simple you can easily make your own pattern. All you really need is a yardstick to draw the straight sides and two different-sized glasses or jars for rounding off the heels and toes. Some people give handmade Christmas stockings in time for a child's first birthday, before the child is old enough to really understand what the present is or to remember who gave it, without being reminded. This is a present that has a much greater effect if given when the child is about four years old. Something for Santa to fill up every Christmas—oh, boy!

6
A Tree to Grow with

FAKE CHRISTMAS TREES have been a growth industry for years, and there's good reason for it. A fresh six-foot Douglas fir imported from Oregon that costs $24.95 in Daytona Beach, Florida, will put you out a hundred dollars or more in New York City. A lot of people don't want to deal with the mess, the increased danger of fire, or the specter of the fresh tree tied to the roof of the car appearing ever more prominently in the rearview mirror with each passing half mile. And when you come right down to it, you can pick up small branches, bare of leaves or any other greenery, following an autumn storm, and at the right moment anchor them in a big container, string them with lights, and put on a few brilliant red and green and gold ornaments, and you have a Christmas tree; the authors have done it in hard times.

But there is something about the smell of a fresh tree that is intoxicating. Every child should know that smell, and there is a way to make sure they do, even though there is every good reason for the household's main tree to be artificial. Give a child who's five to ten years old a live potted fir tree for his own room. Decorate it yourself, or give the child a few miniature ornaments with which to do his or her own decorating. After Christmas, the tree can be planted in the yard—or given to the block or neighborhood association to be planted on public property. It's best to get a tree of this sort from a local garden center, although Plow & Hearth offers a fully decorated live Alberta Spruce for $19.95 in its holiday catalog, while Gardener's Eden has a slightly taller undecorated tree for $20.00.

7

It Doesn't Have to Be a Poinsettia

POTTED PLANTS OR bulbs are never out of place as a Christmas gift, except perhaps to gardeners so avid that they have their own greenhouses. For the rest of us, a plant in bloom or bulbs that we can watch develop into full flower over the next few winter weeks can lift the spirits and help banish the "lows" that so many people, especially in northern areas where the days are very short, are afflicted by.

The classic Christmas plant is, of course, the poinsettia; the classic bulb, the amaryllis. Do not give these to people with indoor cats, however, since the leaves of both are poisonous and can cause serious problems for the curious cat that decides to nibble on them. Besides, there are many other possibilities. For presents that are to be hand delivered, it only makes sense to visit a local florist or garden center, but for friends or relatives across the country, the major garden catalogs are a splendid source. All have perfected the business of packaging plants so they arrive in superb condition. They will not send a plant before it is ready, but are very reliable about sending a greeting with the gift-giver's name advising of later shipment.

The Smith and Hawken catalog carries a considerable assortment of plants and bulbs, complete with planters or forcing bulbs for $14 to $21, including not only such bulbs as hyacinths and freesias, but also herb collections, a living ivy "kissing ball," and a handsome rosemary topiary plant. (The company also features everything from candles to soaps to Christmas ornaments.) White Flower Farm offers some unusual choices such as primroses, oxalis, and miniature amaryllis. Gardener's Eden and John Deere also have possibilities, although their emphasis is more on garden accessories and planters than on plants themselves.

8

Advent Calendars: A European Tradition

ADVENT CALENDARS ARE a European Christmas tradition that goes back to the Middle Ages, and their roots can be traced all the way to pre-Christian Norse celebrations of the winter solstice. In the Christian tradition, each day of the approach to the birth of Christ, from December 1 through December 24, is marked off on a special calendar. There are many different ways of approaching an advent calendar. We know a woman who as a child cut out twenty-four stars or Christmas trees and colored them, and then put them up on a bulletin board, removing one a day throughout the month, as Christmas approached.

These days, reusable Advent calendars are featured by many museums and catalogs. Some involve simply opening a tab on a large pictorial Christmas scene, be it a tree or a Victorian shop, which reveals a new scene underneath each day. Others are more complex and include a miniature object in its hiding place, to be hung on the tree, set up on a table, or left in place to be admired. Some Advent calendars are essentially secular, revealing nutcracker soldiers, miniature sleighs, snowmen, or Christmas trees. Others are overtly religious, and provide figures to be added day by day to an evolving crèche scene.

The particular designs offered tend to vary from year to year, but reliable sources are the catalogs of the Metropolitan Museum of Art, Past Times, and Lillian Vernon.

9
Hark, the Herald Angels Sing!

BARBRA STREISAND, PLACIDO Domingo, Ray Charles, George Strait, Crystal Gayle, Leontyne Price, Willie Nelson, Marilyn Horne, The Temptations, the Mormon Tabernacle Choir—is there anybody who can carry a tune who hasn't recorded a Christmas album? Well, yes, The Beatles and The Rolling Stones, to name a couple of holdouts. But not many famous singers can resist—it's just a matter of time before we get something called "A Rapper's Christmas" from one group or another.

Even people who never go to church are moved by the old Christmas carols, and the popular favorites like "White Christmas," "Rudolf the Red-Nosed Reindeer," and "The Little Drummer Boy" will never fall out of favor, either. Recordings of Christmas carols and songs are always a good gift, especially to families with kids between the ages of five and ten. Listening to a good Christmas album together has a bonding effect on all present, and the recordings are inevitably brought out again as each new holiday season gets into full swing. There's a lot of variation in the quality of Christmas albums, some sounding thrown together, others quite sensational. At the moment, our favorites would be Jessye Norman on the more classical side, and Gary Morris on the more popular side, but that's really up to you. There's a lot of choice out there and even lesser efforts have a way of getting under people's skins and bringing on at least a few goose bumps.

10
Just Nutty About Christmas

THE OLD PHRASE describing a grand dinner as progressing from "soup to nuts" usually puzzles many people these days when we serve a bowl of nuts with drinks before the meal. But in the Victorian era, the Christmas feast would conclude with the passing of a great bowl of nuts, in their shells, with each guest provided with a nutcracker and tiny nut pick or two-pronged fork to extract the fresh nut meats from their shells. A lot of people still carry on this tradition, which is why you will see piles of various kinds of nuts in their shells at supermarkets during the holiday season.

But for gift giving, it has become a custom to send fancy mixtures of roasted nuts, often packed in tin boxes. Probably the best known purveyor of nuts in this country is Jane and Harry Willson's Sunnyland Farms of Albany, Georgia. Their catalog is titled Pecans, Plain and Fancy, and Other Nuts and Fruits. If you're looking for pecans, this is *the* source. They are sold in various grades and sizes, either in the shell, shelled but raw, or roasted and salted. They also carry every other kind of fancy nut, as well as items like chocolate pecan bark, dried fruits, cakes, and cookies. Toasted nuts can be had either salted or unsalted, and there is a sufficient price range so that you can send one fancy tin or a combination of attractively labeled clear bags for under the $25 limit.

Other good mail-order sources for nuts include Mauna Loa Macadamia Nuts. Macadamias are the only nuts they sell, but they make their way into all kinds of candies, cakes, and other confections; dried fruits and coffees are also offered. Because macadamias are the most costly nut there is, you won't get as much bang for your buck here in terms of quantity, but there are plenty of tantalizing choices that would undoubtedly be well received.

Two other companies that sell not only nuts but also a considerable range of other products are particularly worth checking out for their exceptionally handsome gift tins as well as the bounty they contain. The Squire's Choice of Langhorne, Pennsylvania, and Almond Plaza of Maumee, Ohio, both have many possibilities for well under $25, including fancy popcorns, candies, and dried fruits.

11

Spicing Your Own Pecans

YOU COULD ALSO prepare batches of spiced nuts at home for Christmas gift giving. Pecans work particularly well because they are soft enough to absorb flavors easily. The following recipe is not especially time-consuming and the results are absolutely addictive.

SPICED PECANS
Makes 6 ounces

2 tablespoons vegetable
   oil
2 tablespoons butter
1 teaspoon ground ginger
1 teaspoon paprika

1 teaspoon allspice
1 tablespoon salt
1 6-ounce package
   raw shelled pecans

One six-ounce package of raw shelled pecans will fit nicely in a single layer on a cookie sheet.

Place two tablespoons of vegetable oil and two tablespoons of butter—forget the margarine, this is a Christmas present—on a cookie sheet and place it on the middle rack of a preheated 325° oven.

For each six ounces of pecans, prepare a mixture of the ginger, paprika, allspice, and salt.

When the butter on the cookie sheet has melted, mix it well with the vegetable oil and add the 6 ounces of pecans, spreading them out in a single layer. Sprinkle the pecans with half the spice mixture. Toast for 5 minutes. Remove the cookie sheet from the oven and turn and mix the pecans with a spatula. Sprinkle the remaining

24

spice mixture over the pecans and return it to the oven for an additional 4 minutes. Remove pecans and spread on paper towels to absorb excess oil. When pecans have cooled slightly, taste one and add additional salt and/or paprika if desired.

12
Christmas for Our Feathered Friends

FOR THE BIRD-lovers on your Christmas list, a particularly thoughtful gift is a decorative wreath or basket containing birdseed that can be displayed indoors to start with and then put out for the birds to eat. (Some bird-lovers may put it outside the kitchen window right from the start.) Miles Kimball carries a remarkably reasonable birdseed wreath, eight inches in diameter for $7.98, which the catalog suggests should be left out even after the seeds are consumed, so that the straw base can be utilized for nest-building in the spring.

Gardener's Eden features several birdseed decorations. A sunflower wreath—the entire head of a dried sunflower (over eight inches in diameter) is further decorated with millet, barley, seed grasses, and cracked pecans, so handsome that it really demands to be enjoyed indoors before it's turned over to the birds—is only $14.50, an exceptionally good buy for this kind of decoration. There is also a Scandinavian-style swag of seed grasses at $11.00, and a pair of eight-inch star birdseed ornaments for $12.50.

A handsome refillable bamboo basket for seed could still be hanging in the yard next Christmas—$21.50 from John Deere. And if you want to get down to basics, Duncraft, which specializes in bird feeders and seed (including "squirrel diversions"), is the place to look for every kind of feed as well as small bird feeders that are well within our $25 limit.

13
Plush Toys

PLUSH TOYS ARE beloved by young children, and many are hung on to for years, until they become so dirty that parents feel they must hatch elaborate plots to retire the ancient ones to a high shelf or even throw them out (Heaven forfend!).

The best mail-order source by far for plush toys is Whale Gifts from the Center for Marine Conservation. From dolphins to penguins to sea otters to polar bears, this catalog is over-flowing with cuddly cuties. It even has a mommy turtle with three baby turtles concealed inside her. Prices are reasonable, with only a few as high as $17.

REI (Recreational Equipment, Inc.) has a smaller selection of particularly charming plush toys, small in size but beautifully designed, for $18.00. A special winner is Barney the purple dinosaur, $21.95 from Just for Kids. And Lilly's Kids features a wind-up elephant plush toy that raises its trunk and wiggles its ears, at only $12.95. Finally, you can't get much cuter than the rabbit dressed in overalls and cap taking a break from it all in his own hammock (with suction cups for hanging); $18.50 from John Deere.

14
Hand Puppets for Kids

THESE THINGS ARE really cute. How could any child resist a hand puppet ladybug, whose legs are manipulated with your fingers? Or a glow-in-the-dark firefly of essentially the same construction? There are also some nice jack-in-the-box—type hand puppets, including an adorable green worm with a red beret that pops out of a red apple, and a reindeer that goes up and down a red chimney. These puppets are available respectively from National Wildlife Federation, The Nature Company, Toys to Grow On, and Lilly's Kids, all for under $17.00, with the reindeer only $9.98.

A note of economy here: Several hand-puppets are available from more than one company, with price variations that sometimes amount to several dollars. Comparison shopping is in order here, and it would be wise to check out your local toy store so as to avoid shipping costs.

15
Gloves of All Kinds

GLOVES! ANOTHER OF those traditionally boring gifts. Not these days, thank you. How about white cotton knit gloves from The Music Stand with a choice of two-dozen musical instrument embroidered appliqués at $9.95 a pair? Or, for handling roses, green gloves from France, made of a treated cowhide that won't stiffen when wet—with the added attraction of a tan forearm gauntlet to ward off thorns ($19.50); and supple but snug goatskin gardening gloves ($15.00), both from Gardener's Eden. Or maybe you know someone who would be more interested in high-cuffed leather gloves for handling firewood, whether loading it or turning burning logs in the fireplace. They're $14.95 from Plow & Hearth.

Is there a golfer on your list? Think about the "tackified" golf glove made by Neumann, with a palm that gets tackier when wet to prevent slippage, offered by Herrington for $18.95. Then there are "Armodillos" gloves from John Deere, made of the same Du Pont material used in bullet-resistant police vests ($15.00). We could go on at length, but let's conclude with the extraordinary variety of gloves and mittens from REI, designed for many special uses and available in a range of brilliant colors, from navy to purple and back again through emerald and jade.

Gloves boring? Certainly not.

16
Empty-Slate Presents for College Kids

RIDDLE: HOW CAN you thrill a college student by giving him or her a boxful of things with nothing on them?

Answer: When the box contains blank audiocassettes, videocassettes, or photographic film.

As many people know from difficult personal experience—and all of us should be aware of just by picking up a newspaper now and again—the costs of sending a son or daughter through college these days are astronomical. There is likely to be little money left over for extras, or even for things like blank cassettes or film, which have become an integral part of this technological age of education. Send several good-quality tapes or rolls of film to a college kid on a tight budget and you will get a world of thanks. And it's not as impersonal a present as it might seem on the surface. After all, the recipient gets to fill all those empty plastic strips with sights and sounds that express his or her own personality. It's a present that says, "Here's something to help you order your world in your own way." You can, of course, add in a box of cookies to make it seem more festive in your own mind.

17
A Personalized Anthology

SOME OF THE most delightful gifts either of us has received in recent years have been personalized audiocassettes and videotapes. Each of these is, in essence, an anthology. If you have a cassette tape deck with a built-in dubbing feature (which is becoming standard even on lower-priced models) and a good collection of audiotapes, it is really very simple to put together a tape of "greatest hits" or "favorite opera arias" that's entirely of your own devising. Technical perfection isn't the point here. A slightly longer pause between selections than normal, or the occasional electronic squawk between songs isn't going to bother the recipient. It's the thought that counts.

Does someone have a favorite song, say Stephen Sondheim's "Send in the Clowns" or Andrew Lloyd Webber's "Memories"? Both songs have been recorded by dozens of artists, and the avid music fan is likely to have several on different full-length albums. Put together three or four different versions of just a few songs and you have a very special gift. You can also simply put together your own "hits" collection of The Rolling Stones or Luciano Pavarotti. It's a personal gift, not something you're trying to sell, and it's none of the recording industry's business.

Instead of audiotape, if you're going to put together a videotape gift of this kind, of course, you need to have two VCRs—which presupposes you are among those who do indeed know how to operate the critters. Put together a Christmas video, with short scenes from famous Christmas movies and cartoons. Try to be surprising, leaping from Bing Crosby singing "White Christmas" to Jessye Norman singing "Silent Night" in a cathedral. All it takes is one blank tape, some imagination, and fifteen minutes here and there over a period of days or even weeks. Assemble a Humphrey Bogart or Elizabeth Taylor tape, or all the best bits by Peter Lorre—whom many of his contemporaries in Hollywood regarded as the best actor in the business, no matter how funny he looked. After all, the real point of this kind of present is to give a personal twist to material that can be seen only by watching—or listening to—many hours of material. An anthology, personally assembled, can often show how very special certain artists really are. And you will be thanked for a unique present.

18
Surprising the Movie Buff

WHEN SOMEONE HAS a passionate interest in a particular subject, it's always nice to give that person a present that in some way plugs into that interest, be it baseball, classical music, or gardening. A gardener can be easily taken care of—so many of the loveliest plants are annuals, which need to be started afresh each year. But people who amass their own collections of things related to their passion are tough to buy for simply because the chances of duplicating something they already have is so high. And there's nobody harder to stay ahead of than a movie buff.

Movie buffs tend to put together vast collections of old movies on videotape, many of them recorded on their VCRs at three o'clock in the morning, when the fan is sound asleep. Unless you have access to someone in the household who can swear that a given old or new film is not already in a given collection, you are asking for disappointment by guessing. You could, of course, ask the person to give you a list of movies he doesn't have, and pick one from it, but there is another way to manage something a bit more surprising.

What you need is a catalog from Script City of Hollywood. This company offers copies of scripts for thousands of movies and individual segments of television series. Many of them are priced at $24.95, just under the wire of our book's title, if you don't count shipping, and some are even higher. But they also carry a lot of material for under $20.00. Several hundred scripts for Academy Award winners and nominees are $19.95 each, ranging from *Born Yesterday* (1950), to *2001: A Space Odyssey* (1968), to *Who Framed Roger Rabbit?* (1988). Single-episode TV scripts are only $16.95, and range from *Gilligan's Island* to *Hill Street Blues*.

Script City also carries movie posters, lobby cards, and stills. Some of these are rare collectors' items carrying high prices, but there is also a selection of reprints at modest prices. There are several dozen reprints of movie posters at only $12.95 each; still photographs (all 8-by-10-inches: black and white, $7.95; color, $12.95), and lobby cards. These last, reproductions of small ads displayed at theaters, are perhaps the most intriguing. Full-color 8-by-10-inch lobby cards are $14.95 each. One of the nice things about lobby cards is that considerable trading goes on among enthusiasts of these pieces of movie memorabilia, so even a duplicate will simply give the collector a chance to do some bargaining to obtain something else—say Disney's *Lady and the Tramp* for Orson Welles's *The Lady from Shanghai!*

19
Chocolate Heaven

WHAT WAS THE most important gift of the new world of the Americas to the old world of Europe? In terms of basic sustenance, wheat, corn, and the potato obviously rank at the top. In terms of flavor and multiple uses, the tomato would probably get the nod. But a great many people would secretly think of something else even as they spoke aloud a politically correct word like *wheat*. What they would really be thinking would be *chocolate*. Chocolate and more chocolate.

In both big cities and smaller resort meccas around the country there are many splendid chocolate shops that make their candies on premises and do not do a mail-order business. Some of these shops produce chocolates that are as good as you can get, and if you live near one, you already know where to do your Christmas shopping. But for those who aren't fortunate enough to have a local purveyor of high quality, the mail-order choice is wide. Godiva has in the last decade become the most widely distributed high-quality chocolate company in the United States, with "boutiques" located in cities across the country and a large mail-order business. Many people turn to Godiva for gift giving not just because of the quality of their chocolates but also because they offer many kinds of spectacular packaging. You pay for that, of course, which puts a number of their catalog selections over $25, but there is still plenty to choose from at lower prices.

Two famous old companies with superb chocolates are See's of San Francisco and Karl Bissinger French Confections of St. Louis. Both companies have very fair prices for the quality of their luscious products. A newer company that is becoming a favorite of many people is Ethel M. Chocolates, based in Las Vegas but with shops throughout Nevada, Arizona, and California. Their catalog particularly features their butter creams, and with good reason. This is a rare mail-order company that will allow you to put together your own assortment—a nice touch.

If you want to give a present that combines chocolate with nuts, Mauna Loa, Almond Plaza, and The Squire's Choice all provide a number of chocolate-covered goodies. The Squire's Choice carries one particularly unusual item—chocolate-covered espresso beans, which have a lovely crunch and give off a wonderful little jolt of coffee flavor.

As a final thought for the kids, Toys to Grow On has a chocolate-candy-making kit for children, with six trays of candy molds, sucker sticks, sucker bags, candy cups, foil wrappers, a gift box, and instructions.

20
A Basket of Special Treats

At ONE TIME or another, most people have received, and most people have given, a basket or box of foodstuffs for Christmas. These can range from fruit to a selection of jams and jellies, from fancy nuts to a variety of cheeses and spiced sausages. There are numerous mail-order companies that specialize in such presentations. Some of these, including Harry and David, Swiss Colony, and The Wisconsin Cheeseman, advertise so widely that their catalogs may be all too familiar to possible recipients of a gift from you. Thus, while their under-$25 gift assortments are nicely presented and of good quality, it seems wise to check out other possibilities.

Two other companies whose catalogs are becoming increasingly common in mailboxes, Pepperidge Farm and Wolferman's, nevertheless offer items that are sufficiently different to seem somewhat more special. Pepperidge Farm naturally focuses on its cookies and other confections, but some of these, such as the Cinnamon Finger Pastries (¾ of a pound in an attractive holiday tin box for $17.50) are pleasantly off the beaten track. And don't overlook their assortments of fancy soups—there are several under $25.00—especially when thinking of a retired couple or individual on a tight budget. Knowing there's a can of lobster bisque in the cupboard next to the store-brand cream of chicken can be a definite upper. Wolferman's wide variety of gourmet English muffins or crumpets would also be a nice thought for senior citizens (or anybody, for that matter). The company provides a good variety and a considerable range of samplers, including choose-your-own options, for $11 to $21.

If you want to be more personal, put together your own selection of gourmet treats. These might be particularly appreciated by people who live in small cities and towns where the kinds of gourmet shops common in major cities are simply not to be found. A jar of exotic mixed peppercorns in several colors, a packet of dried mushrooms from Asia or Europe, a bottle of raspberry vinegar, a box of Arborio rice from Italy, and a ceramic jar of rose petal spoon sweets from Greece—and you have the makings of a very special present. You can pack them in an inexpensive straw basket from China or just wrap them individually and put them in a nice box. There are many companies that offer exotic gourmet fare, but the standout is G. B. Ratto & Company of Oakland, California, in business since 1897, which offers both exceptional variety and the best prices around.

21
I Have My Own Bag, Thank You

AT THE SUPERMARKET these days we get offered a choice of "plastic or paper" by the grocery packer. But to many this is a "none of the above" kind of choice. There are all the problems with the biodegradable resistance of plastic—but, on the other hand, those brown paper bags come from trees. Statistics show that of the world's largest cities, Rome has one of the lowest levels of nonfood garbage. Why? Because the age-old use of string bags when going marketing persisted long enough to become environmentally chic.

String bags are showing up in many catalogs these days, among them National Wildlife Federation and Hold Everything. A pair is generally $10 to $12. National Wildlife also carries a canvas tote bag with the words PART OF THE SOLUTION in a repeated pattern (two for $17.95). Hold Everything has bright nylon shopping bags with a zipper, in blue, green, or red. An exceptionally attractive hand-woven tote from Guatemala is offered by Christian Children's Fund for $21.95. And Winterthur has a beautiful floral chintz tote for $24.00.

String bags and tote bags for everyday shopping are clearly catching on in this country and the variety available seems certain to increase as time goes on.

22
Buying for Home Handymen

A LOT OF HOME handymen tend to take the fun out of buying them a gift. Their wives are informed exactly what Mr. Fixit wants for Christmas some time in late October, down to the model number. Of course, it's always possible to purchase a secondary gift that's a surprise. But what to choose? A good local hardware store would seem the logical place to look, but this can be a somewhat daunting proposition. There are so many things on the shelves whose exact purpose is quite mysterious. And while hardware store clerks are usually terrific at finding what you need if you can explain to them what it is you want to accomplish, they aren't terribly patient with that ultimate browser's question: "What does *this* do?"

This is an area in which mail-order catalogs can be a real lifesaver. There are pages of gadgets, each one pictured and described. Since home handymen love gadgets that hold things in place, twist them around, puncture them, or drive things into them more easily, it shouldn't be difficult to pick out something of this sort—once you are aware of what the thing you saw at the hardware store actually does.

Three catalogs that could be useful in this area are Brookstone's Hard-To-Find Tools, Edmund Scientific, and Herrington. The last puts the emphasis not so much on tools as on gadgets, from automotive to sporting, and Edmund Scientific also carries lots of science-oriented toys for kids.

23
A Harbinger of Spring for the Gardener

HOWEVER MUCH THE true gardener may love Christmas, the passing of the holiday season means also that it is that much closer to the time when he or she can get back outside and start planting for a new blooming season. For such a person, a small wicker basket full of packets of unusual seeds could be just the thing. Most people are well acquainted with the major seed companies such as Burpee Seed Co. and Park Seed, but we'd like to suggest an alternative: Shepherd's Garden Seeds of Torrington, Connecticut. This is a relatively new company that is fast becoming a favorite among serious gardeners.

What makes Shepherd's special? First, owner Renee Shepherd seeks out unusual seeds from Europe and Asia that are often unavailable in this country. Second, the descriptions of the flowers and vegetables the seeds will produce are both detailed and charming little essays that are a delight to read on their own. But perhaps most of all, this is as elegant a catalog as you will find—of any kind. Filled with exquisite drawings of flowers and vegetables that are printed in a distinctive brown ink, and including numerous recipes, it is a joy to peruse. The same drawings by artist Mimi Osborne decorate the seed packets, giving them a very distinctive look. (Many gardeners would not think of just tearing open a packet of Shepherd's seeds—instead, they carefully cut them with scissors in order to preserve the packet.) The company also offers two handsome cookbooks ($9.95 each) as well as postcards, T-shirts, and a poster print, all featuring Ms. Osborne's splendid drawings. A combination of seeds and one of these latter items would make a very special gift for any gardener.

24
What Cooks Always Want More Of

A FIRST-RATE COOK of either sex is always running into a problem: the people who say, "I'm not sure I dare invite you to dinner." The truth is that good cooks like good food; it doesn't have to be fancy. But many people are intimidated, and they feel the same way when thinking about the possibility of giving a good cook a Christmas present connected with the kitchen. The assumption is that the good cook already has everything. But there are a number of items that can be given to your "gourmet" friends that will be sincerely welcomed, things that regularly wear out or that a few more of are handy to have.

Here are some of the possibilities:

- Wooden spoon sets, which tend to discolor.
- Oven-proof sets of ceramic or terra-cotta bowls that can be used for everything from onion soup to salsas.
- Potholders and tea towels: They tend to get badly soiled or burned or generally threadbare in even the best-run kitchens. Give new ones that are attractive but not so fancy that they look like they ought to be preserved under glass.
- Pepper grinders: The pepper grinder that doesn't eventually start delivering nearly whole peppercorns hasn't been invented yet.

25
Much-Talked-About Cookies

HOMEMADE COOKIES ARE a traditional way of saying Merry Christmas without spending a fortune. Their freshness and the care that is often taken in hand-decorating them is quite enough to make them special. A nice tin box or wicker basket is all that is really needed in way of presentation, but one way to make such a present a little more glamorous is to deliver them on a small glass or porcelain platter picked up at an antique store or flea market. There are a lot of inexpensive "finds" out there if you keep your eyes open.

Many people regularly bake up batches of cookies for holiday giving and have their own time-honored recipes. And the home and food magazines always offer new varieties in preholiday issues. The recipe that follows is named in honor of one of Lily Tomlin's funniest one-woman skits in which she plays a teenager who repeatedly demands that her parents (whom she also plays) "please stop talking about that cake." People will tend to go on about these cookies, too. They are not cookies with a holiday theme, but offer all the rich delectability the holidays call for.

"PLEASE STOP TALKING ABOUT THOSE COOKIES" COOKIES
Makes about three dozen

½ cup all-purpose flour
½ teaspoon baking soda
¼ teaspoon salt
¼ teaspoon powdered ginger
½ cup butter

½ teaspoon vanilla extract
1 tablespoon brandy
½ cup light brown sugar
¼ cup white sugar
1 egg

1¼ cup oatmeal, un-
cooked (quick or old-
fashioned, not instant)
½ cup macadamia nuts,
chopped in blender or
food processor—some
chunky bits should re-
main

1 cup (6 ounces) butter-
scotch morsels

Preheat over to 375°. Combine the flour, baking soda, salt, and ginger in a small bowl and set aside. In a larger bowl cream the butter with vanilla, brandy, and sugar until fluffy. Add the egg and mix well. Beat in the flour mixture gradually. Stir in the oatmeal and macadamia nuts. Finally, add the butterscotch morsels and mix again. Drop the mixture by teaspoonfuls about 3 inches apart on an ungreased cookie sheet, preferably nonstick. Bake 8 to 9 minutes for a chewy-crisp texture. Allow the cook-ies to rest about 3 minutes before removing from cookie sheet.

26
It's in the Cards

ANYONE WHO PLAYS bridge, poker, or canasta regularly will always be delighted with a gift of playing cards. Cards wear out, become flabby and difficult to shuffle, and a couple of bent corners can give the game away. There's an enormous variety of playing cards available, from formal ones personalized with initials, to elegant ones reproducing great works of art, to novelty cards that can add extra humor to a nonserious game. Just stay away from the novelty cards for those who regard their bridge game as central to their sense of self.

New playing-card designs are introduced regularly, but some that particularly caught our attention in recent catalogs suggest that these companies can be counted on as a good source. Miles Kimball, which carries a host of inexpensive novelty items and household gizmos, will personalize two decks of cards with either a full name or initials for a mere $7.49. At that price, you might consider adding in one of their novelty decks, like the set with "Make Checks Payable to . . . [whatever name]," or their Christmas cards with reindeer, snowmen, elves, and Christmas trees as suits ($3.49 a pack).

The Museum of Modern Art features a striking set with contemporary graphic faces designed by Takenobu Igarashi. A double deck from Winterthur has face cards decorated with oriental figures drawn from nineteenth-century illustrations in its rare-book collection ($12.95). Of historical interest are the reproduction colonial playing cards offered by Treasures from Your National Parks ($5.95 per pack) and the presidential set of playing cards from Smithsonian ($15.00). For those who collect unusual playing cards, Past Times has a $12.50 deck reproducing fifty-five great paintings of nudes by the old masters, and Flax Art & Design has an extraordinary set of cards created by fifty-six different contemporary British artists ($16.00 per pack).

27
T-shirts Galore

IT'S THE AGE of the T-shirt, and since no one can have too many of them, they make excellent gifts. There are, of course, T-shirt shops all over the country where you can get whatever message you want printed, but a lot of these places have a tendency to overcharge, failing to reveal hidden costs until after the shirt has been printed. Happily, there are numerous terrific mail-order sources.

Some of the most amusing T-shirts around are available from The Music Stand, a catalog that specializes in gifts related to the performing arts. Anyone you know who is studying music or dance or is an amateur or professional performer is likely to get a kick out of T-shirts with such slogans as: MU-SICIANS ARE SOUND PEOPLE, DANCERS "TURNOUT" BETTER, I KNOW THE SCORE, or ALMOST FAMOUS. The company will print any of over a hundred slogans and designs not only on T-shirts for $12.95, but also on baseball caps ($7.95), mugs ($6.95), cotton nightshirts ($15.95), or a canvas tote ($10.95). Another company with amusing shirts is What On Earth, which has a series that depicts a human brain, its areas appropriately labeled for a doctor, lawyer, golfer, or tennis player ($14.95), as well as a wide range of other designs.

The Public Radio catalog called Wireless, and the Public Television catalog Signals are both big on T-shirts, with choices appealing to many different interests at $15 to $20. And for the nature lover in particular, the World Wildlife Fund, National Wildlife, and The Nature Company all carry very attractive wildlife T-shirts, with prices ranging from $11.95 to $17.95.

On the other hand, you might want to make a T-shirt yourself. Dover Publications carries a series of iron-on transfers in full color of North American Indian and Celtic designs, intricate Victorian flower patterns, seashells, and carousel animals. Each 8½-by-11-inch volume contains from forty to over one hundred patterns, and the cost is only $2.95 per volume. If you have an artistic bent, Enterprise Art of Largo, Florida, carries an exceptional selection of fabric paints and pens, as well as items ranging from sequins to sew-on mirrors in a variety of shapes and sizes. This company offers thousands of craft items and can fill an order for several-dozen small items with amazing speed. Their prices are just about unbeatable, too.

28
Reasonable Clothes for Kids?

THE MAJORITY OF catalogs for children's clothing that show up in the mailbox are likely to give heart palpitations to most people looking for something cute to give a grandchild, niece, nephew, or godchild. Not because the clothes are so attractive—and many of them are—but because the prices are so high. As one first-time grandmother recently muttered, "I didn't realize we were into Paris originals for six-year-olds."

Fortunately, there are some exceptions. Land's End Kids is full of straightforward clothes in snazzy colors, from a mock-T dress for girls to polo shirts for boys, that come in well under our $25 limit. These are very appealing clothes, cut in traditional styles but in the very bright colors and offbeat color combinations so popular with today's kids. Less conventional, almost costumelike clothes at good prices are available from Just For Kids. Some of these clothes really are costumes, like Superman and Batman sleepers, at prices ranging from $15.50 to $16.95, depending on size. Just For Kids also carries a variety of toys and accessories at reasonable prices.

Some clothes for infants and toddlers are offered by One Step Ahead and The Right Start Catalog, although both these sources focus more on child-care products that would appeal to safety- and convenience-minded parents. For infants, of course, it's perfectly acceptable to give a care item in the name of the child even though the parents will be making use of it.

29
I'm Sorry It Isn't a Coat — But It Is *Sable*

SABLE COATS ARE widely regarded as the *ne plus ultra* in the now very controversial realm of fur coats. Any painter will tell you that sable brushes are the best for subtle coloration, and so will women who take special care with their makeup. The smoothness with which sable brushes lay on cosmetics, especially over the cheekbones—we are informed by reliable sources—is simply not to be equaled.

Sable makeup brushes are not to be found in your average pharmacy. You'll have to go to a full-scale cosmetics department in a major department store. These brushes are not cheap, but you can certainly put together a small package for under $25 that will delight a special lady, and you have our permission to put the title above on the gift card. Every array of Christmas gifts should contain a little joke or two.

30
Masters of the Barbecue

EVEN THE MOST conscientiously macho American male feels perfectly safe being seen stirring a sauce or wielding a spatula around the barbecue grill. And since barbecuing is a form of cooking that lends itself to the proliferation of gadgets and accessories, there are a lot of potential Christmas gifts that are bound to be welcomed by a master of the grill.

Although barbecue equipment and fixings show up in many catalogs, this is another of those cases where a single source will more than serve. The Grill Lover's Catalogue from Char-Broil is an absolute cornucopia of barbecue-related gift items. It has more marinades and sauces than you can shake a long-handled fork at. With names such as Texas Gunpowder, Margarita Sauce, Praline Mustard Glaze, Burgundy Marinade, and Soy-Ginger Sauce, there are at least a couple-dozen to choose from. Many are sold individually, others are parts of sets that go beyond our $25 limit, but there's no reason you couldn't order one of these and break up the set into presents for two different people on your list.

The company also sells every kind of charcoal briquette and wood chip imaginable, including a two-pound bag of wood chips made from twenty-five-year-old white oak barrels used to age Jack Daniel's Tennessee sipping whiskey, for $6.99. And when it comes to gadgets, the gamut is run from four-prong spit forks ($4.99) to a revolving hot dog/sausage wheel ($9.99), as well as individual steak thermometers ($7.99) and a one-handed salt-and-pepper mill so you don't have to put down your tongs ($12.99). If there's a barbecue gadget you can't find here, it probably hasn't been invented yet.

31
Remember When?

BOTH AUTHORS OF this book recall hot summer days, in Texas and Massachusetts, when there was nothing quite so welcome as a glass of lemonade served in brilliantly colored, jewel-tone aluminum tumblers that stayed really cold in your hand. Well, they're back, a set of 6 costing $21.95 from Community Kitchens of Louisiana. The company also offers 6 aluminum straws for $6.95, or a set of 6 tumblers and 6 straws for an under-the-wire $24.95. Dessert dishes in the same line are 6 for $21.95. Among other items making a comeback are shiny stainless-steel martini shakers, with a strainer lid, $19.95 from Crate & Barrel.

In another area, Christmas tree bubble lights have reappeared (after long eclipse by Italian minilights), $12.98 for a set of 7 from Miles Kimball. Even madras, totally out since the mid-sixties, is beginning to crop up again, in a set of 8 tea towels from The Pottery Barn ($20.00). These items are surely just the beginning of a trend. What goes around, comes around.

32
Playthings of Yesteryear

IN THIS TIME of Nintendo games and ferociously hyped fads like the Ninja Turtles, it can sometimes seem as though most children have migrated a few years ahead of time to some bubble-city on Mars. But some of the toys those of us over forty recall from our own childhoods have held their ground. The Slinky, for example, that fascinating metal coil that could negotiate a stairway with the aplomb of Fred Astaire, never went off the shelves completely and can even be found at outlet-store chains these days. Some of the other favorites of the thirties, forties, and fifties seemed on the verge of disappearing for good, but in the last few years a lot of them have been making a comeback, perhaps because we're dealing with children so used to television that it is possible for them to become bored with it.

Many catalogs that include children's toys are likely to feature at least a few of the old-time favorites, but there is one source that specializes in them, Back To Basics Toys. Remember Raggedy Ann and Andy? Here they are at $15 or $22, depending upon size. How about Lincoln Logs or the original Tinkertoys? An intermediate set of the former is $20, a super set of the latter just $24. Back To Basics carries the original Etch-A-Sketch for $17, too. There are also toys of more recent vintage, including, of course, dinosaurs. But what makes this catalog such a pleasure for those of us of a certain age are the memories it brings forth. How about an original hardcover copy of *The Little Engine That Could* at $5.95 to take you back?

33
Save Those Quarters

AT A TIME when the savings accounts of adult Americans are at record lows, it may seem to be tilting at windmills to give a child a "piggy bank," in the hopes of encouraging the savings habit. But the times may be changing, and certainly some of the reproduction antique mechanical banks in recent catalogs should appeal to any youngster.

Miles Kimball has two such reproductions of nineteenth-century banks. One is a cast-iron elephant, enameled bright blue with a gold-colored saddle. A coin placed in the trunk will be flipped into the opening in the saddle when the tail is pulled. A second bank, also cast iron and painted by hand, has a barrel, a clown with a hoop, and a little black dog. Put a coin in the dog's mouth, pull a lever, and the dog jumps through the hoop to place the coin in the barrel. Each of these banks is a reasonable $14.98. Another antique reproduction, from The Paragon, has a mama and baby frog. A coin placed on the baby's belly (he's lying on his back) will be caught and swallowed by mama ($22.50).

If you prefer something more modern, Childcraft has a transparent money vault with a secret combination for $13.95. Since it comes with play money, coins, credit cards, and a checkbook, this one could be fun for the budding entrepreneur. Savings banks for kids do seem to be making a comeback.

34
Transforming the Director's Chair

ONE OF THE most ubiquitous pieces of furniture to be found in the apartments of those just out of college—in their first apartment, starting out on their adult lives—is the director's chair. They are attractive, surprisingly comfortable, and the better-made ones are remarkably sturdy. They are also affordable to those taking on their first full-time job. (You'll also find them in the apartments and homes of extremely successful people—who either just plain like them or appreciate the fact that they can be folded up and put in a closet.)

Because director's chair covers do tend to wear out, anyone who has them will appreciate replacements. Plain covers in a variety of colors are available in many home furnishing stores across the country. But keep your eye out for more fanciful creations, including geometrics, Native American designs, jungle animals, or a rain-forest parrot. They have cropped up in a wide range of catalogs recently, and never run more than $21.95. Especially reasonable covers are available from Home Decorator's Collection.

35
Mobiles and Kites

THEY TAKE LIFE with a breeze. They must be assembled by the recipient from cardboard and wire or paper and balsa wood. And while a kite's first purpose may be to soar above a field, it can make just as spectacular a room decoration as a mobile. They make especially good presents for teenagers, college students, and people furnishing their first apartment.

Wildlife mobiles are all the rage these days. Take your pick from tropical fish (Smithsonian, $16.95), spiders and insects (The Nature Company, $16.95), tropical parrots (National Wildlife, $16.95), or a variety of sea creatures (Whale Gifts, $22.50). In a slightly different vein, Bits and Pieces has a cut-and-assemble mobile of Saint George fighting off four different dragons at once ($12.95).

Mobiles are to be found in many catalogs year-round, but kites are more of a seasonal offering, in the spring and summer. Designs also change from year to year. But a steady source for kites is Into the Wind, of Boulder, Colorado. If you're thinking of giving a kite primarily as a decorative present, stick to the flatter ones that would dress up a large bare wall. If you're giving it to people who are sure to test it out on the beach or a nearby park, look for aerodynamics.

36
Hey, That's Really Big!

THIS PARTICULAR ENTRY goes under the heading of "I wish I'd had those when I was a kid." We're talking about inflatable toys. The champions in this category are certainly the large and remarkably realistic animals developed by The Nature Company. Anyone who has ever been to one of their stores in the past six years will have seen these creatures flying overhead and lurking in corners. There's a Tyrannosaurus rex dinosaur that's 30 inches high for $19.95; a mountain gorilla of the same height and price; either a 24-inch mountain king snake or a 40-inch common king snake (gulp!) for $9.95 each; a 51-inch-high emperor penguin for $24.95; and perhaps best of all, a pteranodon with a 91-inch wingspan for $19.95. Wow!

Then there are the inflatables to get physical with. Toys to Grow On has a 33½-inch-tall inflatable "Bop-A-Robot," which has a weighted bottom, so that he pops right back up no matter what a kid does to him ($14.95). Learn and Play offers great-big action balls, a 21-inch red one for $19.95, and a blue 25-inch for $24.95 (the even larger yellow and green balls are more expensive). Or how about a snow tube from Lilly's Kids, 34 inches wide with a recessed seat and handles on the sides, sturdy enough to hold up to 250 pounds—an excellent alternative to expensive wooden sleds at only $17.98.

37
Paperweight Delights

PAPERWEIGHTS WERE FIRST made in ancient Egypt, but it was not until the mid-nineteenth century that the great glassmakers of France began to produce the extraordinary objects now seen in museums. By the end of the century, however, they passed out of fashion and did not begin to make a comeback until the end of the 1950s. Art glass paperweights are now produced in many countries, the finest examples often costing several hundred dollars. But there are some handsome glass paperweights, as well as brass and polished stone ones, available for under $25. There are many people who collect paperweights, but even for the noncollector, they make an excellent present.

A very popular paperweight that has turned up in several catalogs is a globe of the world in clear and frosted glass, simple but elegant. The best price we have seen on this is $17.98 from Lillian Vernon. A green apple paperweight in leaded glass from The Nature Company is $18.50. Whale Gifts features both a whale and a dolphin in iridescent glass ($20.00 each).

A handsome polished jasper sphere on a carved wooden stand from Smithsonian is listed at $22.00. For the brass lover, Lillian Vernon has two possibilities, a pair of 1¼-inch-square dice, weighing 9 ounces each, with a velour drawstring gift pouch, are $17.98, and a brass 7-ounce star, with initials, is $9.98. And, carrying the initial idea to its logical conclusion, the Initials catalog offers a $15.00 brass paperweight in the letter of your choice, unless your name is something like Quentin or Xerxes—a few letters are not available.

38
Surprise Box for Book and Design Lovers

FOR THOSE ON your Christmas list with an interest in books and the decorative arts, there is a single source that will make it possible for you to put together a gift package that is a virtual cornucopia of goodies. The source is Dover Publications of Mineola, New York, a company that specializes in reprinting classic works of literature, architecture, design, and science, as well as Victorian and turn-of-the-century full-color labels, stickers, postcards, gift-wrap designs, and cut-and-assemble projects of many kinds. Their publications are beautiful and so reasonably priced that one sometimes wonders how they do it.

A pair of recent Christmas packages, for example, were put together for a mother-daughter team who run a shop of antiques and fancy gifts—hard people to buy for. Each of their Christmas boxes contained the same kinds of things, but entirely different examples of them. Each received two kinds of "Old-Time Stickers" booklets. These are pressure-sensitive reproductions of designs from a century ago, 23 to 28 full-color peel-off-and-stick-on beauties per booklet, each booklet with a theme: Christmas, Valentine, Easter, and Halloween stickers, as well as floral, cat, and patriotic themes. At $1 per booklet, they are perhaps the best buy mentioned in this book.

The two ladies also received, tied up together with these stickers in a small bundle, different examples of Amish quilt and Christmas gift labels. Again for $1 each, these striking peel-and-stick designs are 2 by 3 inches with ample writing space. The next layer in the box contained two examples each of Dover's sensational giftwrap papers. Each set, in a sturdy, full-color shrink-wrapped 9-by-12-inch folder, contains four different 18-by-24-inch sheets as well as heavyweight matching gift cards. The patterns range from antique Christmas designs to classic Scottish plaids, from Chinese floral to Art Nouveau butterflies, along with cats, dogs, and even dinosaurs. These are the kinds of gift papers it's hard to let out of the house, but at only $2.95 a set, you can order some extras to use in craft projects.

The packages for the mother-daughter antique-shop owners were finished off with reprints of the *Victorian Sourcebook of Medieval Decoration,* with 166 full-color designs ($9.95), and *Bloomingdale's Illustrated 1886 Catalogue* ($8.95). Price: under $20.00 for each surprise box—received with many *oohs* and *aahs* and a fondly anticipated disagreement about whose package had the better stuff in it.

These gift packages do not even begin to suggest the treasures in the Dover catalog. What would you like? Authentic Shirley Temple paper dolls ($3.95); a cut-and-assemble Southern Plantation or House of Seven Gables ($3.95); collections of piano pieces, from classical to ragtime, in a range of prices; or perhaps a Tiffany stained-glass coloring book ($3.95)? Or choose from any of dozens of classic works of literature, from Dickens to Whitman. Dover has it all.

39
Everyone Needs Coasters

FEW HOUSEHOLD ITEMS seem to lead a harder life than coasters. Especially during summer months, even the best-made coasters begin to betray us by coming up with the glass or beginning to curl or come apart. As something that regularly needs replacement, they will always make a welcome gift.

Coasters are very widely available, so here we will stick to a few of the most interesting we saw in recent catalogs. For the flower lover, a set of laminated, cork-backed reproductions of botanical prints from The Paragon (6 for $13.50), or 100-percent-wool needlepoint designs based on 1759 prints (4 for $18.00) might be especially welcome. Baseball fans would certainly be delighted with early baseball coasters from The Metropolitan Museum of Art (6 for $16.50). Off the beaten track are reproductions of European manhole covers from The Museum of Modern Art (a set of 12 for $15.00).

On the sturdier side, consider brass coasters with hand-engraved animals, made in India (a set of 6 only $9.95) from the Christian Children's Fund; or Crate & Barrel's green marble coasters with cork bottoms (6 for $15.95). One of the nice things about coasters is that you can find something for almost any taste.

40
Dressing Up the Table

IN THESE RUSHED times, a set of handsome placemats on the table can go a long way toward making a meal seem more elegant and leisurely. Genuine cotton damask placemats with a woven-in flower design set in red and white or blue and white squares from Voice of the Mountains are advertised as being able to stand up to repeated washings over many years (4 for $23). The Smithsonian offers special Christmas placemats with a scalloped embroidered border of red ribbon, green Christmas trees, and wrapped packages (a set of 4 for $18). For a couple without children, a pair of striking handwoven buntal fiber placemats from The Museum of Modern Art, at $10 apiece, might be just the thing. They come in natural, rust, and black designs.

Our favorites, however, are the laminated mats from The Metropolitan Museum reproducing nineteenth-century cannery labels. These are exceptionally colorful and engaging. One set features labels for corn, string beans, tomatoes, and peas; the other, pears, cherries, blueberries, and grapes (sets of 4 for $14.95). These are simply knockouts.

41
A-Tisket, A-Tasket

WHAT ARE THE best bargains available today, in catalog after catalog, store after store? Woven baskets. They come from India and Africa and South America and the Philippines and the American Southwest and above all, from China. Many are handsome enough just to display by themselves, as room accents. Others are just made to hold dried or artificial flowers. Some are splendidly utilitarian, instant organizers of the miscellaneous. And because they are often so inexpensive, they can also serve as a special container in which to present a gift of some importance.

Woven baskets show up in a great many catalogs, but the best sources we have seen are Lillian Vernon and Williams-Sonoma. Lillian Vernon always carries a variety of useful baskets in her ever-changing catalogs, but there are almost always two or three offerings that people are most likely to put out on display. For example, we ordered a set of four nesting baskets made in China in handsome dark browns with lighter accents, each basket with a bulbous bottom and narrower banded top. People always admire these and simply shake their heads in disbelief when they are informed that the set of four cost $14.98.

Williams-Sonoma quite naturally specializes in serving baskets, to hold anything from popcorn to fruit to bread; some of these are more specialized, as in a rattan basket and accompanying handblown glass bowl that will hold three quarts ($22). There is always good variety at reasonable prices to be found here.

On a more specialized note, Miles Kimball always seems

to have special seasonal baskets, like a trio of nesting reindeer baskets (the largest 8 inches long and 9½ inches high) for only $8.49. And King Arthur Flour features round, square, or baguette baskets made of ash, each with a British-made tea towel in a green-and-white pine tree pattern ($18.95 each).

42
Helping Others Around the World

GIVING TO THE needy has always been an important part of the Christmas spirit, and one way to do it is to select gifts from one of the catalogs whose aim is to provide employment for craftspeople in Third World countries, support college scholarships, or help hungry children.

Oxfam America and the Christian Children's Fund both have Christmas catalogs that offer stunning crafts from around the world. Handmade boxes, jewelry, musical instruments, and textiles are all available, the majority of them well under $25. In the United States, beautiful objects are crafted by Navajos and offered by the Southwest Indian Foundation. Some of the turquoise and silver creations are expensive, but there is still a considerable amount of small jewelry, ceramics, and Christmas ornaments that are affordable. Berea College of Berea, Kentucky, founded in 1855, has a catalog of wood, ceramic, and textile crafts, ranging from cutting boards and yo-yos to exceptionally attractive fireplace brooms and walking sticks. No student at Berea pays tuition; instead, they work in 120 different departments. The crafts in this catalog pay the tuition of their creators—and the objects themselves are absolutely professional.

Finally, don't forget UNICEF, which offers ceramics, ornaments, books, and puzzles as well as its famous Christmas cards and notepaper.

43
A Gift in Your Name

ONE OF THE salient aspects of Christmas is the generosity we can show in helping others in need. A fine way of doing this is to make a gift to a charitable organization, whether it's engaged in fighting cancer, heart disease, AIDS, or supporting disabled veterans or hungry children around the world, and asking that a card be sent to someone we know stating that a gift has been made in his or her name.

But there are some serious etiquette problems lurking in the background here, as any reader of "Dear Abby" will be well aware. First, we would suggest never making this kind of "in your name" gift for anyone who clearly doesn't have the financial ability to do the same. Someone who has worked overtime for two months in order to put together any kind of Christmas at all is not going to appreciate this gesture of generosity toward others. That's simply human nature.

Second, never make an "in your name" charitable gift to one son and daughter-in-law, while giving something tangible to another son and daughter-in-law. Even if one son has pots of money and the other not much, to discriminate between them in this way is asking for trouble.

Third, don't get huffy if you don't receive a thank-you note. A lot of people will have trouble saying the right words. We've heard several people say, "What's going on here— doesn't she think we can be generous on our own?"

All in all, "a gift in your name" can be splendid in some circumstances, a problem-maker in others. Think carefully about it.

44
What's in a Name?

MOST PEOPLE LOVE things with their names or initials on them. There are, however, a minority who hate the whole idea, so be sure you know who you're dealing with in this regard. For those who do like initials, many companies offer at least some items that can be personalized. But there are also several companies that specialize in this area.

As its name implies, The Write Touch focuses on stationery, notepads, desk and travel diaries, and the like. As is generally true, the stationery considerably exceeds our $25 limit, but the notepads and diaries are affordable. A couple of their more interesting items include an album that holds 200 postcards acquired on trips or from friends ($20), and boxes of 100 personalized self-stick shipping labels for $17.

The catalogs called The Personal Touch and Initials are both from the same company, the latter carrying a number of more expensive items. In either catalog, you'll find everything from mugs with either initials or first name to canvas tote bags to a folding gold-plated shoehorn with up to three initials ($14.95, $19.95, and $12.95 respectively). One rather charming gift is a wicker basket in the shape of a scallop shell containing 10 bars of small initial soaps for $19.95.

Finally, don't forget Lillian Vernon, whose ever-changing catalogs always contain numerous items that can be personalized.

45
Serious About Their Game

IT IS RARE to come across a general-interest catalog that doesn't offer a lot of attractive and/or amusing gifts for golfers and tennis players. T-shirts, caps, coffee mugs, jewelry, you name it, it's available. Most golfers and tennis players recognize that there's something a little obsessive about their love for either sport, and they are perfectly willing to be teased a little and even genuinely amused by a present that pokes some gentle humor. Give them that mug or T-shirt.

But think twice about presenting them with cute versions of the tools of the sport—tennis balls with initials or a cute saying, initialed golf balls, or neon tees with funny comments. After much experimentation, even amateur players have usually arrived at a strongly held decision about what kinds of golf or tennis balls work best for them, and they won't play with any other brand. If something new comes on the market, they might give it a try, but that's something they want to decide for themselves.

If you know a player well enough to be certain exactly what brand of golf or tennis ball he or she uses, fine; the recipient will be delighted with such a present. But don't give a non-name brand just because you can get it initialed. Save the cuteness for off-the-course, off-the-court gifts.

46
The Frame Can Make the Picture

Is THERE SOMEONE on your Christmas list who is a fine amateur photographer, a watercolorist, an accomplished needlepointer, or a person who likes to mount dried flowers on hardboard backings? Such people are always in need of frames for their work—and a really special frame may even inspire them to create the perfect work to complement it. While even smaller cities will have a few such shops, custom framing can be an expensive proposition. Large cities will undoubtedly have major art-supply stores, on the order of Flax Art & Design, which is also a good mail-order source (Flax sends out several small catalogs each year but its full-size annual spring catalog costs $8), but there is a company called Graphik Dimensions Ltd. that specializes in frames and should be of particular interest to those looking for a great Christmas gift for an artistic friend.

Graphik Dimensions Ltd. carries a wide range of sectional, custom-made, and preassembled frames in both wood and metal. The sectional metal frames come in as extensive a range of colors as we have seen anywhere, several-dozen shades, and even includes a line of semiprecious-stone look-alikes, including malachite, amethyst, and rose quartz. One can order these sectional frames in pairs (sides) of any length from 5 inches to 48 inches. If you wanted an 11-by-18-inch frame, the first pair would cost $7.50 in a malachite design, the second pair $11.50, for a very affordable total of $19.00. Every frame comes with all the assembly hardware needed, lucid instructions, and is very easily put together.

The wooden frame offerings from Graphik range from rustic to baroque designs, and include some exceptionally handsome ovals. A preassembled oval baroque frame, 12 by 16 inches, costs only $17.95, with a rectangular rustic design of the same size at a mere $12.95. A custom-made frame in a carved Florentine design would come to $21.70 for the same dimensions. Overall, these are frames that cause guests to ask where you got them, and if you state their prices, most people find the amounts hard to believe.

47
Hand-Painted Wooden Frames

A WOMAN WHO HAS been a close friend for a very long time always sends us a profusion of small presents at Christmas—nothing particularly expensive, mostly little surprises that she has been gathering since the previous January. Because she travels from New York to the midwest almost every year to spend Christmas with a gathering of family, we send her three or four nice but lightweight things, almost always including a piece of antique junk jewelry, which she loves, and at least one item that has been made at home. Before Christmas last year, she asked if the heaviest of her presents could be opened before the trip, or should it be taken with her? After Christmas, she reported that she was glad we had told her to take it with her, since it made quite an impression.

What was it? From an outlet-store chain, a $3 wooden frame that had been handpainted, layer by layer, over a period of several days. Before you say,"I couldn't do that," hold on a minute. One of the authors of this book is an accomplished artist, while the other couldn't draw his way out of a paper bag. But it was the latter who hand painted the frame. If you have a sense of color, some patience, and a willingness to experiment, be assured you, too, can pull this off.

Before starting to hand paint a wooden frame, decide what basic hue you want to predominate—whether green, red, blue, or yellow. Then start by spray painting the frame with an enamel of that color. If you want to end up with something in a pinkish tone, still start with red; for violet to purple, still start with blue. The frame will need two of these base coats.

Now you start playing. You will need several items. First, a sponge. A natural sponge is best, but a plastic sponge with good-size crevices will do fine. Get one of the big brown ones available at any supermarket, the kind you can tear pieces from with your bare hands. You will need some small paint brushes—nothing fancy, just one of those 99-cent packs kids buy to take to school. Also get hold of a little container of white typewriter correction fluid, the kind you apply with a self-contained brush. And if you'd like to get an iridescent look, pick up a couple of appropriate shades of frosted nail polish in the sale bin at your local pharmacy.

As to paints, water-base enamel hobby paints, available in small jars at most hardware stores, and some water-base tempera paints school kids use, are all that's needed, although you might want a small jar of gold leaf, too. Later on, if you find this kind of thing fun, you might want to expand your palette by ordering some small jars of paint from a craft supply company like Enterprise Art, which has a very wide choice.

Put a newspaper down on a table, get a few small plastic cups with a little water in each, and start in. Using a small piece of sponge, dab on one color all around the frame. Let it dry, then paint in some white with your correction liquid, making lines and little dabs. Sponge more lightly with a different color, let it dry, and add in some more squiggly lines with a brush or some nail polish. If you feel things are going wrong, stop and do some more light sponging the next day. When you get a result you think is pretty, you're finished.

The object here is not to make the frame look like it came from the same quarry as the marble columns in St. Peter's in Rome. All you want is something nice. Let everything dry thoroughly and then give the frame a couple of coats of clear acrylic spray. You'll feel like a genius, and will have recaptured your childhood at the same time. It's a nice feeling. And it makes for a much appreciated present.

48
Encouraging the Beginning Artist

ALMOST ALL CHILDREN like to make pictures when they are young, whether they develop any mature artistic talent or not. Drawing stick figures, splashing purple paint on the supposed cow, making the grass bright orange—it's all a part of exploring their new world. For that very reason, crayons, markers, watercolors, and water-base tempera paints are always a good bet as a Christmas present. You can easily put together a grab-bag surprise box of such art materials from your nearest chain outlet store—just be sure to wrap each item separately before putting it into a bigger box, thus making one present much more exciting.

Any general children's catalog will have various art supply kits for kids, and they show up in a lot of other mail-order sources, too. The emphasis here is on the word *kit*. That means there is some organizing feature, be it a miniature chest of drawers, a see-through briefcase, or a plastic crayon dispenser. The idea is that these containers will encourage children to pack their coloring materials up and put them away when they've completed their masterpieces. This seems to work with a minority of children, but there are an awful lot of adults, too, including many of the most famous artists in the world, who haven't the slightest interest in this kind of neatness. It is, of course, worth a try.

The widest variety of beginners' art kits we've seen are those available from two sources: Childcraft, and Toys to Grow On. And when considering this kind of present, don't forget rubber-stamp kits featuring animals, flowers, and the like, or the multicolored stickers that kids are so wild about these days. Both are widely available.

One special item we came across deserves mention. The

Nature Company has an elaborate 16-by-58-inch poster of the rain forest and its creatures, with black outlines on a white background for $16.95. It comes with 24 coloring pens and it seems likely older children, who are ready to take the line boundaries seriously, could produce their own ecological "masterpiece" and have an awful lot of fun in the process.

49
The Secret of Remaindered Books

To SOME, THE idea of giving a remaindered book (marked down in price because of overstock) as a Christmas present seems tacky. Others fear that the recipient will already have the book. Yet some of the nicest under-$25 presents we have received have been remaindered books, and some of the most appreciated presents we have given to others have been, too. But there are some simple rules to keep in mind when considering a gift of this nature.

Let's deal with the "tacky" business first.

We're not talking here about making a present of one of last year's best-sellers. We're talking about exceptionally beautiful books that were once as expensive as all get-out, in the $45-to-$75 range. There are people who buy "coffee-table" books on art, architecture, the formal gardens of Europe, the history of movies or Broadway, celebrations of classic cars or great sailing ships of past centuries when the volumes first make their appearance. Those who have piles of such books scattered around (or artfully displayed), whether they bought them for show or because they really want to read them or need to have them for professional reasons, are obviously not candidates for this kind of present. But very few people buy more than one or two of this kind of book a year, and most will be thrilled to receive something they never would have bought for themselves because of its cost, and won't care in the least what you paid for it. A treasure is a treasure.

Now, on to the question of how to choose something that the recipient doesn't already have.

First, stay away from the big piles of remaindered coffee-table books in major bookstores or their mall chain outlets. Go instead to second-hand bookstores. Again, avoid anything in

piles. Go to an individual section—say, gardening or architecture. You will find mostly used books, but among them, there
are likely to be a few copies of various books that are brand
new. These will be books that the big stores and chains didn't
want to handle because there were too few of them. Second-
hand bookstores pick them up because they want to stock as
wide a range as possible of books on a given subject.

If a book has been published abroad, in England for
instance, you are another step ahead of the game. A local
second-hand bookstore in Daytona Beach was the source of
two splendid volumes last Christmas. Both were books related
to gardening, one a collection of exquisite botanical drawings,
most in color, made by several different women in the same
family in nineteenth-century England; the other was a book of
ravishing photographs of "secret gardens" in Paris. Both gifts
were big hits.

By far, the best catalog source of remaindered books in
the United States is Daedalus Books. You won't find best-
sellers or run-of-the-mill coffee-table books here. What you will
find are beautiful books at remarkable prices. Like the good
second-hand bookstores, Daedalus buys up limited-quantity
books that are often very special. If you see something you
think would make a good gift, order it immediately, because
some of the best treasures will be quickly snapped up and you
won't find them in the next catalog. If the company has run
out of stock, you will get a refund check attached to your order
slip. Deadalus is a first-class organization all the way.

50
Bookmark Beauties

THE TRUE READER usually has several books going at once—a best-selling novel, a favorite classic in the process of being reread, a nonfiction book that is best taken a chapter at a time. For such people, bookmarks are always an appreciated gift.

There are a number of very attractive bookmarks available these days. Condé Nast's Portfolio has been featuring an intriguing trio of gold-plated brass bookmarks in the form of famous chair designs—Louis XVI, Chippendale, and Bentwood ($22.00). The Music Stand has an extraordinary selection of 39 different musical instrument bookmarks at $3.95 each; these are also gold-plated. A pair of cloisonné butterfly bookmarks from Winterthur are a shimmering buy at $10.00.

While bookmarks are great for finding your place, there is another problem readers encounter: trying to keep a heavy book open to the correct page while you take notes or check another source. Levenger's has a splendid solution to that problem in the form of an 8½-inch tan leather strip with lead weights at each end, and page-gripping suede on the bottom. Very handsome, too ($19.95).

51
'Tis a Puzzlement

THERE ARE THREE main kinds of puzzles with untold numbers of devotees. There are mechanical puzzles, like the infamous Rubik's Cube; pictorial jigsaw puzzles; and crossword puzzles. Curiously, these different kinds of puzzles seem to appeal to different kinds of people; there is surprisingly little crossover of interest. We don't really recommend giving books of crossword puzzles as Christmas presents, simply because the real fans are always picking up such books for themselves. But ingenious new mechanical puzzles turn up year after year, and the range of jigsaw puzzles knows no bounds, featuring dozens of new possibilities annually.

Let's consider mechanical puzzles—their very names are fun. Take the Devil's Staircase, which you try to take apart, and the Vexahedron, which you try to put together; or Quicksilver, a round maze with a mercury "player," not to mention Lunatic, this time, interlocking wooden pieces. All these are from Bits and Pieces, none is more than $20 and most are under $15. Over at World Wide Games, we found a dozen "Tavern Puzzles" involving interlocking metal pieces that you couldn't possibly take apart—or could you? They have names like Satan's Stirrup, Dirty Dog, Sneaky Pete, unless you want to step up to Double Trouble. Each of these is $13.95. World Wide Games has lots of other possibilities, too, but, frankly, we'd rather retain our sanity.

52
You Hold, I'll Glue

THE RANGE OF kits that makes it possible to take a boxful of diverse pieces and put together a three-dimensional object has never been better. These are some of the most engaging and sometimes challenging gifts on the market. And there's something for everyone, from the preschooler to the advanced hobbyist.

For example, Constructive Playthings has a set of brightly colored star-shaped plastic pieces that fit together on all sides to make innumerable formations. Designed for two-to-five-year-olds, the set costs $14.95. A preteenager and parent could enjoy working together on one of the architectural kits from Flax, such as the Tower of Pisa or the Duomo of Florence. Printed in full color on heavy coated paper, numbered pieces are put together to build an architectural masterpiece. Each kit also includes a complete history of the monument ($23.00).

Both the Art and Artifact catalog from Barnes & Noble and The Museum of Modern Art offer a fascinating 54-card picture deck created by the designers Charles and Ray Eames in 1952. Each 3½-inch card, depicting "familiar and nostalgic objects from the animal, vegetable and mineral kingdoms" has six slots on its various sides, making it possible to build a vast number of different formations from this "House of Cards" ($18).

The Classics in the Making catalog from Mason & Sullivan has a great variety of kits for hobbyists of all kinds. Some are very expensive (although not for what they are) but there are a number of possibilities in the under-$25 category. For example, there is a kit of gliders—assembled by cutting and gluing—that offers fifteen examples, including the famous *Voyager,* requiring about two hours' assembly for each ($16.95). They also feature a die-cut model of wood and molded plastic of the *Spirit of St. Louis* that will hold a hobbyist enthralled for forty hours ($21.95).

53
Organizers for Neatniks

WE ALL KNOW a few neatniks, people who seem always to have everything organized, put away, labeled, and generally shipshape. How better to please such people than to give them something else to aid in their endless quest for perfect order?

The catalog for neatniks is without question Hold Every-thing. This company lives up to its name, with a box, bag, or other container to get almost anything better organized, in any room of the house, not to mention your car. People who are relatively neat but can live with a little slack around the edges may find some of the items in this catalog quite amusing. Any genuine slob will probably break out in hives and start gasping for breath after about three pages. But it does have everything.

The classiest boxes around come from Exposures. From floral designs to "faux croc" (odile), marbled to paisley, these boxes are a handsome lot, and almost all are under $20. They are primarily intended for photographers, but they could be used for stashing a lot of other things out of sight, too. Other good sources for organizing items are the art supply companies Flax and Dick Blick.

54

Elegant Notecards

NOTECARDS FOR CHRISTMAS? How boring can you get!

OK, so it may not be something *you'd* be thrilled to receive, but you'd be surprised how many people would, especially women over sixty who were raised in a more gracious era and have retained some of its niceties. We regularly receive notes from godmothers, aunts, or close friends of our late parents. One of the good things about notecards is that they allow people to send greetings and a little news without having to go through the process of writing a full-scale letter. Yet, they have about them a degree of grace and refinement that a postcard—the preferred form of communication among many of the younger people who bother to write at all instead of reaching for the phone—simply doesn't convey.

Really attractive notecards are not cheap, and for someone who uses them a lot, a gift of a boxed set can be much appreciated. Many major museum catalogs carry generous selections of notecards reproducing works of art in their collections, with blank interior pages. The holiday catalogs of The Metropolitan Museum of Art and the Museum of Fine Arts, Boston, for example, carry page after page of boxed notecards, not including several additional pages of Christmas cards. Ranging from Impressionist paintings through Dutch flower paintings, American quilts, and on to Japanese-lacquer reproductions, there is something for every taste. A couple of standouts from The Metropolitan were a set of 48 notecards, 4 each of 12 subjects, featuring exquisite reproductions of nineteenth-century hummingbird lithographs by British artist John Gould ($16.95); and stunning Tiffany windows at the same price. Up in Boston, 8 different Aubudon Ducks in a box of 32 were $9.95; even more exciting are 30 die-cut fan-shaped notecards reproducing

6 antique fans from the museum's textile collection ($11.95). These last were a terrific hit with a godmother who has an early December birthday. For Christmas, one could always combine two different boxes of the lower-count designs and still stay under $25.00.

55
Jingle Bells

FROM THE PEAL heard at Salvation Army posts in shopping districts, to the singing of "Jingle Bells," to the great tolling of church bells on Christmas Eve, Christmas is a season of bell sounds. Bells in various sizes and degrees of tintinnabulation are available anywhere Christmas ornaments are sold. Many catalogs feature jingle bells of various kinds, from wreaths of bells to Scandinavian woven doorknob decorations with bells attached.

But you also might consider taking the notion of bells a little further afield. There are quite a number of garden bells on the market now, for hanging outside the kitchen window or on the patio. Smith and Hawken has been offering handsome cast-iron bells in the form of flowers with a cricket in bas-relief (2 for $16), and pine cone cast-iron bells that would be terrific on the Christmas tree (a set of 6 for $16). Over at Gardener's Eden, there are cast-iron bells in the shape of pine cones and flowers (3 for $10, two sets for $16), and a trio of delightful enameled bells in the shape of a tomato, an oriental cucumber, and a green pepper ($12, or 2 sets for $20). Any of these could spend the holiday season in the house and then be moved outdoors.

56
Chiming in the Wind

DESPITE THE LETTERS to "Dear Abby" from irate neighbors complaining about the incessant noise from the yard next door, wind chimes continue to be very popular. They make a nice present to anyone with a sizable backyard. On hot summer days, their tinkling can make it seem several degrees cooler.

Several we have thought particularly attractive in a visual sense appear in various recent catalogs. A metal hummingbird in a circle of flowers with a pewter look were $19.95 from National Wildlife. REI was offering a flock of miniature cast-iron birds for $17. Enameled cast-iron snow pea pods from Gardener's Eden are a delight ($19). The catalog from Robert Redford's Sundance has only a few items that cost less than $25, but one of them is an eye-catching wind chime with copper-finished bells hanging from three tiers of horseshoes suspended from chain link. And at only $16, the 20-inch chime seems quite a bargain.

You should also take a look around local craft shows, where there is often a booth featuring wind chimes, manned by the artist, who will be more than willing to fill you in on the history of these visual and aural treats.

57
For the Budding Musician

A NUMBER OF THE children's catalogs offer plastic musical instruments for very young children, from two years and up. It is claimed that most of these will make melodious noises no matter what the kids do with them—but since kids are going to make a racket anyway, anything even approaching music seems like a step in the right direction. The Smart Toys Catalog has an accordion ($20.95) and a xylophone with case ($18.95). Over at Hand in Hand, you can find a bright-yellow trombone and a red violin ($21.95 each). More realistic-looking shiny silver instruments from Learn and Play include a trumpet, a saxophone, and a clarinet ($9.95 each, all 3 for $24.95). Learn and Play also features a variety of musical videotapes for the very young, including four *Sesame Street* thirty-minute tapes and a song-lyric poster for $14.95 each.

Although most of the instruments it offers are for older children and beyond the $25 limit, *the* source for videos and audiocassettes for children is Music for Little People. They've got everything across the board in terms of musical interests and ages. There are Raffi tapes (with songbooks) featuring twenty or more kids' favorites on each tape ($10.98 per set); for older kids, there are cassettes of music from Leonard Bernstein's *Young People's Concerts* ($7.98). How about a cassette of lullabies from Broadway musicals, from *The Sound of Music* to *Les Misérables?* Or the Parents' Choice Award recording by Bill Harley called "50 Ways to Fool Your Mother"? These and many other possibilities are under $10. Not only can you find great variety here, but there's also an index of artists and titles, which makes shopping a lot easier.

58
Silly Slippers

COZY, FURRY SLIPPERS in the shapes of animals make great presents for kids—at least up to a certain age. They'll be appreciated by girls from the time they can walk until they are on the threshold of adolescence, but boys sometimes start resisting them around the age of seven. Anyone who has seen the hilarious movie, *A Christmas Story,* will remember the mortification of the young hero at being forced to try on the pink bunny pajamas and slippers sent him by a misguided aunt. But at a younger age, silly slippers can be a great hit with kids of either sex.

Silly slippers are available all over the place, but we simply have to mention the fuzzy bee and ladybug slippers from The Nature Company ($19.95 a pair in three sizes by age). These are just about as delightfully silly as you can get.

59

Fun Socks and Underwear

FOR MOST MEN in their forties and fifties, *the* boring presents of their teenage years were the inevitable brightly wrapped but ultimately disappointing packages of socks and underwear. Only the yearly tie from Aunt Agatha ("Where in the world did she *find* it?") was contemplated with less enthusiasm. But that was in the old days, before socks went psychedelic and Jim Palmer began modeling bright-colored bikinis. Socks and underwear can now make some of the most colorful statements under the tree among the assorted piles of opened presents.

Extra-fancy socks and underwear are, of course, widely available, but for those who like to avoid the malls, the REI catalog offers a wide variety of very colorful socks for both men and women for $4 to $12 a pair. What On Earth is a source for unusual socks, with patterns ranging from golf motifs to Bullwinkle characters to solar system designs. The Music Stand sells white terry-lined socks that can be personalized with any of more than two-dozen performing-arts appliqué logos ($7.95 a pair).

For boxer shorts with a difference, it's back to What On Earth, which has everything from beer mug to buttered popcorn designs, not to mention glow-in-the-dark dinosaurs ($12.95). In the glow-in-the-dark vein, Wireless has white-on-black polka dot as well as Fred Flintstone boxers ($12.50 and $14.95). But the niftiest boxers we came across were a single design offered by the gardening company Smith and Hawken: brilliantly colored and very handsome vegetable garden shorts ($18.00). You never know where you may come across just the right thing!

60
Candy for the Kids

THEY'RE GOING TO get their hands on it anyway, so why not make it fun? How about a gumball machine, for instance. John Deere has one listed as Stingy Gumball Vendor. It doles out the candy little by little from a wooden vendor with an inverted glass jar on top. With a pound of gumballs, the machine is $17.50. John Deere also offers a gumdrop tree—a 15-inch-high tree of natural wood twigs with a supply of gumdrops to be attached to the branches ($22.50). It might even be possible to persuade an older kid that this was a holiday-only treat, to be packed away until next Christmas—well, maybe.

Also keep your eye out for candy kaleidoscopes. These are actual kaleidoscopes for under $20.00 that come with jars of hard candies. You can put candy in the jar that is attached to the tube and enjoy the delightful patterns. The candy will be eaten, of course, but can always be replenished.

61
Laffs, Laffs, Laffs

HAVE YOU A mischievous kid on your Christmas list, the kind who likes to play practical jokes? On the theory that "if you can't lick 'em you might as well join 'em," why not contribute to prankster merriment? Toys to Grow On has a collection of the "World's Greatest Gags," including old favorites like a hand buzzer and a snake that jumps out of a can of nuts: 8 gags for $14.95.

If you want to go further, you can put together a collection of your own from the Just for Laffs catalog from The Fun House. This compendium of silliness has trick soap that turns your face black; a bug in an ice cube; a squirt camera; whoopee cushions of several sorts; and enough socially repellent bad-taste goodies to guarantee a "class clown" blue ribbon. As we all know from celebrity interviews and biographies, class clowns often go on to great success, and your present of a bunch of these items is strictly educational from your point of view. At least that's what you tell the kid's parents when they say, "Really, you're just encouraging his wild streak."

62
It's Magic

KIDS WHO ARE practical jokers are often incipient magi-
cians—a considerably higher calling. Starter magic-trick collections occasionally show up in children's catalogs. Learn and
Play, for example, has a Hat of Magic for $12.95 that includes
a top hat, magician's wand, instruction book, and a good supply
of simple magician's "tools." The catalog suggests this for six-
to-twelve-year-olds, and like other kits of its kind, that seems
off the mark. One of the authors was heavily into magic as a
child, and the tricks offered in this set won't engage any child
over the age of eight. If a kid has any aptitude for magic, he
or she will be dragging a parent to a professional magician's
shop by the age of nine. The clerks in these shops are wonderful
with children—that's what entertaining at a thousand birthday parties will do—and very astute at judging the level of
sophistication the child has attained. The parent may say,
"Don't you think that's too complicated, dear?" about the
wand you wrap in newspaper and proceed to tear into bits,
only to make it reappear intact, but the clerk will say, "I think
he (or she) can handle it," and will be quite correct.

So, if you think a child might be interested in magic, we
would suggest getting a catalog from a company that specializes
in magic tricks, and see what they offer in the way of starter
kits. A couple of well-known ones are Abracadabra Fun and
Magic, and Hank Lee's Magic Factory.

63
Getting a Kid Started on Stamp Collecting

STAMP COLLECTING IS one of the best hobbies a school-age child, seven and up, can have. It fosters neatness and organization, encourages an interest in geography, and the subject matter of commemorative stamps is so varied that a broader understanding of what goes on in the world is naturally instilled. What's more, it's a whole lot of fun.

The best way to get a child started on stamp collecting is not with a small album and a miscellany of canceled stamps, but rather with a selection of first-day covers. First-day covers are now issued with the arrival of each new stamp in most countries around the world. A colorfully illustrated envelope, with the new stamp affixed, is canceled at the issuing site with the first-day-of-issue postmark. The site chosen, at least in the United States, is closely associated with the subject of the commemorative stamp: a state capital, birthplace of an author, what have you. There are a lot of small countries, like Mauritius, that issue stamps celebrating foreign people and events; since a significant portion of the government's income is derived from issuing stamps, such countries are not above issuing a Madonna stamp, although in the United States she'd have to have been dead at least ten years before the matter would even be considered (briefly).

If you want to put together a collection of U.S. first-day covers over the course of the year, your local post office can give you the dates and how to go about it. While this is the least expensive way of doing it, it's also a good deal of trouble. But major stamp companies acquire first-day covers in large quantities, and resell them at a modest markup—at least the most recent ones; rare covers from years ago can cost a small fortune. A Wyoming company called Fleetwood specializes in first-day covers, and they are also readily available from H. E. Harris, Brooks Stamp, and Mystic Stamp. From any of these companies, you should be able to put together a packet of eight to ten covers for under $25.

64
Nature Kits for Kids

THE VAST INCREASE in public awareness of environmental problems and the growing number of endangered species on our planet has led in recent years to the manufacture of many kinds of kits and toys that explore these problems.

There is no doubt that the more children understand about their environment and the enormous variety of creatures with which they share it, the better off we all are. But it's still important to point out that not all the "learning" toys for children are created equal. There is a difference between a "nature" kit that includes only natural forms, and plastic replicas of natural forms. We don't mean to get up on a high horse here: Both kinds of toys have their place, even for the same child. But there is a difference that some catalogs tend to obscure, so let's start with the real nature kits, and then move on in the next chapter to the replicas.

Learn and Play is the strongest catalog we've seen in the area of real nature kits. They offer four kits related to rocks and minerals, seashells, fossils, and gems. Each includes a display tray, a magnifying glass, activity cards or books, and 12 to 26 actual examples of the particular natural form. Each kit is $22.95. They also have a tadpole hatchery and an ant farm, with coupons to acquire the live frog embryos and ants, each at $19.95. We would advise checking with any child's parents first, however, to see how they feel about these latter two gifts—a lot of adults are far more squeamish than kids.

Learn and Play also has a miniature greenhouse set for $19.95 that makes it possible to grow a mixture of flowers and vegetables from Burpee Seeds. Promises Kept features three delightful indoor garden pots that would delight any eight-year-old, an eighty-year-old great grandma, and anyone in between. There is a cook pot in the shape of a chicken that grows preplanted basil, marjoram, and savory; a teapot that is planted with chamomile, spearmint, and lemon balm; and a flower pot, in the shape of a watering can, that will produce edible Johnny-jump-ups, nasturtiums, and anchusa. Each is only $16.95, and all are as charming as you can get.

These wonderful little pots also bring home a point to remember: It's not just in children's catalogs that you will find good presents for kids. Grown-up catalogs often have a few items that any kid would love.

65
Nature Replicated

WHEN IT COMES to creatures that swim through the deep, wriggle and crawl in hidden places on land, and revive the mysteries of the age of the dinosaurs, nobody has got it in plastic like Toys to Grow On. You can get a box of 50 sea creatures, from octopus to stingrays to lobsters; or 70 insects, including an excess of spiders; or 40 dinosaurs, all in colors that go Mother Nature one brighter, from $12.95 to $16.95. For what they are, these are wonderful, and will thrill the gross-out glands of any kid. Just remember that the giant purple octopus or twelve-inch earthworm is bound to greet parents from the headboard early some Sunday morning.

More realistic are the plastic animal sets from Just for Kids. There are insects here, too, a kit of 24 with a set of cards describing the habits of each ($8.95). Very detailed "animal families" with cubs and adults feature lions, elephants, and the like; an 11-piece set is $12.95, a 15-piece set $15.95. Quite beautiful are the silk-screened, poly-filled 4½-inch-long endangered frog species in vibrant colors. Machine washable and suitable even for very young children, the set of 3 is $13.95. A portion of the sale of the frogs goes to the World Wildlife Fund, which itself just happens to have a present that is perfect for Christmas. These are old-fashioned Christmas crackers with a difference: Give a tug at the pull-strip at either end of the package to produce a "pop," then pull out a party hat, a funny note, and a miniature ceramic animal, such as an elephant, polar bear, or other species.

66
Nature Books for Kids

THERE ARE SO many nature books for children on the market these days that it's difficult to see the forest for the trees. But some really do jump out at you. Taking that literally, The Nature Company offers two absolutely spectacular pop-up books, one on bees, the other on butterflies. These inform-ative 9-by-12½-inch hardbound books are truly beautifully made, and a steal at $12.95 each. For younger kids, this resource offers another pop-up book in which each letter of the alphabet is represented by an animal ($14.95). Also delightful is the unbound Animal Shuffle "Book," which offers 104 cards, half of which depict animals, the other half, typical animal activ-ities. There is a correct correspondence between the two groups of cards, but it also allows for endless silly combinations like "the rhinoceros crawled under a rock." Talk about making learning fun, and it's only $12.95.

National Wildlife created a book it calls *The Unhuggables,* which is cheerfully advertised as "yucky," since it concerns everything from skunks to spiders to sharks.

The Northstyle catalog features several stunningly pho-tographed nature books including *Eagles for Kids, Loons for Kids,* and *Whitetails for Kids,* each available in either hardcover ($14.95) or softcover ($6.95).

Exactly because nature books are so common these days, it seems wise to hold back and look for the ones that are really different or particularly elegantly produced.

67

A Breath of Fresh Air

MOST OF THE catalogs offering children's toys, even though they offer many terrific things, come on like gang-busters, with the rat-a-tat-tat of Saturday morning commercials. They feature a dizzying array of possibilities—which can leave anyone going through them feeling somewhat exhausted. But there is a catalog with a difference. It has won the Parents' Choice Seal of Approval for the last three years in a row, and there are very evident reasons why.

HearthSong is not a catalog that seeks to overwhelm but rather to entice. Like all the other catalogs, it has brightly colored illustrations, but they are printed on paper that is off-white (on the verge of a light beige). This gives the entire catalog a much softer feel—and it's much easier on the eyes. Beyond that, HearthSong offers many toys not seen anywhere else, and a far greater number of wooden toys than is usually the case. For example, there are two kits for children to make their own finger puppets, one featuring gnomes, the other, little flower children. They come with wooden bases that look like elongated mushrooms (the rounded top becomes the puppet's head); several colors of felt to be cut into costumes; glue, paints, brushes, and patterns. They're enchanting, and at $14.95 a kit, a bargain as well.

HearthSong is so full of splendid toys, from the nicest Jacob's ladder we've seen (two-inch-square wooden blocks held together by colored ribbon, which perform magical tumbling tricks) to stunning iridescent jumbo marbles, that it's difficult to decide what looks like the most fun. We must issue two words of warning about their most-ordered product, however: Buy extra. The product in question is modeling beeswax in brilliant colors (6 colors for $6.80, 12 for $11.75). The beeswax softens in the hand and can be molded into everything from dinosaurs to flowers (we know, we've made both). This stuff isn't just for kids. Extremely relaxing to use and so pliable that even a total klutz can make something lovely out of it, there's no question it will become a favorite in any household. Once you've finished a creation, the beeswax hardens again for display, but it can always be recycled simply with the warmth of your hand.

68
Ah, the Smell of Baking Bread!

THE ART OF homemade bread seemed on the verge of oblivion only fifteen years ago, but the natural foods movement and increasing public awareness of dietary concerns in terms of health brought it back in a big way. For your bread-making friends, consider the wide variety of specialized tools and bread-making ingredients in the King Arthur Flour Baker's Catalogue. Their flours and meals range from amaranth, used since biblical times, to teff, an ancient African grain, and include all the usuals, from buckwheat to pumpernickel. Whole, cracked, and flaked grains and cereals are also available. And, of course, there are sourdough starters, barley malt extract, seeds from dill to poppy, as well as specialty oils and extracts. One of their most intriguing offerings is a line of concentrated herbal and spice oils in bottles with droppers; these can be used in place of dried herbs.

King Arthur also carries an extensive line of bakery utensils and pans, with special sections in the catalog devoted to cakes, cookies, and muffins, as well as pizza and pasta. Numerous cookbooks are featured, many of them in paperback. From this catalog it would be very easy to put together a package that includes a small cookbook, a range of flours, and a baking utensil—for well under $25.

69
An Array of Trivets

TRIVETS WERE ORIGINALLY three-legged metal stools on which to place pots cooking over the logs in a fireplace. With coal stoves, and the further development of the modern kitchen, trivets with much shortened legs were used to place hot dishes on to protect the dining table. It is almost impossible to have too many trivets—whose meaning has now expanded to include cork or laminated "hot pads"—when it comes time for big family gatherings at Thanksgiving, Christmas, or Easter. They make excellent Christmas presents and there are many highly attractive ones available.

An irresistible solid-brass trivet from Winterthur is in the shape of a nine-inch bow. It's solid enough to take the weight of a very large casserole dish; its short feet are insulated with rubber to protect the table from scratches, and it is certainly handsome enough to display on the sideboard when not in use; quite a bargain at $20. A chrome-plated steel trivet from Italy offered by Voice of the Mountains is an ingenious design that cradles either round or rectangular dishes and is expandable to fifteen inches. Because it has handles, it can be used to carry a hot dish to the table ($16.75).

A hand-carved wooden fish trivet made in Haiti would be especially appropriate for Christmas: The interior of the fish spells out the Greek letters *ichthys,* the traditional symbol of the Christian faith. This trivet, about 6-by-13 inches, is only $13.95 from the Christian Children's Fund.

An intricate iron stand, 8 inches long, is a reproduction of an 1818 original and is a real bargain at a mere $5 from Treasures from your National Parks. Finally, The Wooden Spoon has a set of three cork trivets on wooden bases for $24.50, the largest measuring 8 by 12 inches.

70

The Candles of Christmas

CANDLES ARE INDELIBLY associated with Christmas, and because they are consumed as they light our evenings, they make fine Christmas presents. There's no such thing as having too many pretty candles in the house. While candles are widely available in department and gift stores, there are always some special ones offered in catalogs that you aren't likely to come across just anywhere. Lillian Vernon always features interesting candle holders and candles; special holiday possibilities include 6¾-inch wax stars in bright red, green, and gold (set of 3 for $8.98); and 10-inch dripless tapers in metallic gold, individually wrapped in a storage box ($14.98). White Flower Farm has astonishingly lifelike Bartlett pear candles ($15 a pair, packaged in a wooden box), as well as 12-inch dinner candles made from rolled sheets of honeycomb, providing a unique texture ($14.95 a pair in a wooden box). And Gardener's Eden features charming candles in miniature terra-cotta flowerpots (6 for $8).

Pure beeswax candles are often difficult to come by, and are therefore much appreciated. An excellent source is the Massachusetts company Rent Mother Nature. Its 12-inch beeswax candles in plain and fluted styles burn very slowly, about ninety minutes per inch ($15.95 for 6); also offered are authentic Colonial bayberry candles, nearly 11 inches in diameter, at the same price. This company specializes in gifts that involve "leasing" a maple tree or lobster pots, at prices considerably beyond the range of this book, but there are other reasonable gift possibilities aside from the candles.

71
It's Not Johnny Carson's Fruitcake

JOHNNY CARSON'S FAMOUS assertion, which he's been playing for all it's worth for many years, that there is only one fruitcake in the world that people keep passing on to someone else so they won't have to eat it, may be a slight exaggeration, but it's certainly true that a lot of people really do not like the stuff. There is a company in Texas that sells a fruitcake we actually like, but we're going to keep our mouths shut on this one; even among people who do like fruitcake, arguments about what makes a good one can be fierce.

We've found that a good alternative to fruitcake is the traditional English plum pudding. Perhaps because it is moist and served warm, it appeals even to fruitcake haters. It does require steaming, of course, so don't give it to someone who can't boil water. But it is delicious, and anything eaten by the Cratchits in *A Christmas Carol* has to be regarded as classic holiday fare. Plum puddings are available from several sources, but the one from Maple Grove Farms of Vermont is as fine as any we've come across. A 14-ounce pudding and 7-ounce hard sauce package to accompany it are $19.95.

If you'd like to consider making your own plum puddings as gifts (there are many recipes available), consider acquiring a Cathedral Steamed Pudding Mold, made in Portugal, from Williams-Sonoma for just $13.50.

72
Potpourri Made Special

THERE ARE TWO very different kinds of potpourri: The kind that you put in a pot on the stove or even a specially designed pot that can look presentable in the living room has become a cliché of every discount store in the nation; but really good potpourri, of the sort that is put out dry in small quantities, is expensive stuff. An eight-ounce bag can easily cost up to ten dollars. The good stuff is usually packed in clear plastic bags with labels that are in themselves small works of art. These can certainly be presented as gifts on their own.

But they can also be made more special. Keep a lookout for small boxes made of wood, leather, metal, or even woven natural fibers, particularly at flea markets and small antique stores. It's a plus if the lid of the box will stay open on its own, but it's fine if it needs to be propped against the side. At Christmastime, buy some extra potpourri for your own use and use small amounts of it to fill little boxes you've acquired. Then give a package of potpourri together with the box as a single gift. A nice present has been made more personal and even nicer.

73
Mismatched China?

ABSOLUTELY. FLEA MARKETS, small antique stores, and garage sales are treasure troves when it comes to extraordinarily beautiful china that is available only by the twos and threes, the full set having gradually succumbed to the ravages of two or more generations of the dropsies. Even top-of-the-line brands like Wedgwood and Spode can be picked up for three to four dollars when there are only one or two for sale.

Acquire such plates whenever you see them, and as Christmas nears, see what kind of combination can be put together. Groups of mismatched salad or dessert plates can make for a stunning party table—you see it done all the time in the very best magazines. In fact, there are lines of china being manufactured these days in which no two are alike as a deliberate design statement.

Obviously, this isn't a gift for everyone. But anyone with imagination and flair will be delighted with a gift box containing half a dozen different flower patterns, fruit patterns, bird patterns—whatever you can pull together. One of the tricks in assembling such a present, however, is to make sure that the plates are obviously mismatched. Never put in two of the same design. It's the very difference that counts.

74
Teas of the World

A HANDSOME GIFT for the tea lover can be put together simply by visiting any relatively up-scale supermarket. At our local Publix, they carry the brightly colored boxes of Twinings imported teas, and three lines of herb teas: Celestial Seasonings, Bigelow, and the new Lipton line. A very nice present could be put together by combining some of Twinings breakfast teas (English, Irish, and Ceylon), a couple of their afternoon teas (such as Earl Grey and Darjeeling), as well as a selection of herb teas. While all the herb teas are nicely packaged, those from Celestial Seasonings are particularly festive and amusing: Tropical Escape, flavored with pineapples and oranges, for example, depicts a straw-hatted penguin lolling in a hammock on a tropical isle. Celestial also has the broadest range of herb teas (those of all three brands are naturally caffeine-free), including Raspberry Patch, Strawberry Fields, Country Peach Spice, Cranberry Love, and Cinnamon Rose.

A present of teas could be nicely rounded off with the addition of a package or two of imported cookies, of which there are many varieties available at reasonable prices.

75
Homemade Fruit and Herb Vinegars

FLAVORED HOMEMADE VINEGARS are so easy to make, it's a wonder why anyone spends an extra couple of dollars for the imported ones. Various cookbooks differ slightly in their approaches, simply because there are those who feel the best flavor is developed by using a smaller amount of fruit, cranberries for example, and steeping it longer, while others prefer to use more fruit and let it steep only for a week or two. According to the latter method, the usual proportion is one cup of fruit to one quart of vinegar.

Let's concentrate on a cranberry vinegar, since the fruit has such strong holiday associations, and is readily available from mid-November until Christmas. Simply put 1 quart of vinegar—white, red, or cider—in a saucepan and bring it to a boil. The three different vinegars produce slightly different flavors. Red wine vinegar gives a lovely Christmas color, cider vinegar a more complex flavor. Cranberries are one of the few fruits that are tart enough to require the addition of a teaspoon of sugar to the boiling vinegar. Add ½ cup of the cranberries, and boil for 2 minutes. Then strain the vinegar into clean glass containers to which the additional ½ cup of cranberries has been added. Because of the preservative nature of vinegar, the containers do not have to be sterilized. Let the vinegar steep in a cool dark place for at least a week.

The process is the same for herb vinegars. But it takes only a sprig or two of fresh rosemary or a few leaves of mint or basil to flavor the boiling vinegar. These are then discarded, and the vinegar, after cooling to room temperature, is strained into a container with a couple of springs of the fresh herb. Once again, allow to steep in a cool dark place for a week or two.

What should you use as containers if you want to give fruit or herb vinegars as Christmas presents? We recommend you invest in glass bottles with raised designs imported from Spain. Extremely handsome, such bottles are available in a number of specialty stores and by mail order from both Williams-Sonoma and The Chef's Catalog. Six assorted 20-ounce to 30-ounce bottles cost around $30, but this is another case where two bottles containing your vinegar would make a splendid gift, so that the overall cost per gift would still remain well under $25.

76
Something Different for Grandma

IT'S A PROBLEM Christmas after Christmas: what to give grandma from the kids. Soap, handkerchiefs, or candy picked out by Mom? Here's a different idea.

Buy a good-quality oversized scrapbook at a local art supply or office supply store. And then gradually fill it up in the course of the year with things created by the kids or related to their various activities. Put in a little of everything: drawings made at school or on a rainy Sunday afternoon at home; that hundred-word essay with the nice big red A at the top; photographs of the kids building a snowman, playing under the sprinkler, creating a sandcastle at the water's edge.

Have the kids themselves paste things in—neatness is not the object here. Encourage them to think of things they might like to add to the gradually filling pages. Yes, press some flowers, ferns, or leaves, the old-fashioned way, between sheets of paper towel in the back of a heavy book such as a full-size dictionary or atlas. They'll be ready in four to six weeks, and the kids can use them to make their own designs on two or three scrapbook pages. As Christmas comes nearer, have the kids cut out some brightly colored stars, bells, or trees and create their own Christmas cards right on the scrapbook pages. Or let them do it with crayons or markers. And at the end have them write "Merry Christmas, Grandma," and sign their names.

Grandma will tell them it's the nicest Christmas present she ever received.

77
Audiotapes for Everyone

WITH THE VIRTUAL demise of the long-playing record at the hands of CDs, audiocassettes have taken on a new importance to those looking to give a nice present that can be listened to—whether it's music, comedy, or recorded books. For under $25, you can give someone two audiocasettes, which is almost impossible to pull off with compact discs. An excellent source is Wireless, the Public Radio catalog. They've got everything from Bernstein to Woody Allen, from Jack Benny to Pavarotti. And since the catalog carries many other kinds of gifts as well— mugs, T-Shirts, ties, even candy—it's a useful all-round source.

But if you are primarily interested in audiocassettes, there is nothing like The Mind's Eye. There's a little of everything here. Children's books read aloud? How about Robin Williams's Grammy Award–winning rendition of the tale of Pecos Bill, or Shel Silverstein reading his own *Where the Sidewalk Ends* (each $12.95). Do you remember *The Shadow*? Orson Welles stars in 8 of the original radio mysteries: 6 hour-long cassettes for only $19.95. Then there's the "Canned Laughter" series—each decorative can contains 2 hour-long cassettes featuring Burns and Allen, Mae West, W. C. Fields, and many other favorites ($9.98).

On the more serious side, there are BBC collections of great poems and dramatizations of everything from *The Odyssey* to *Pride and Prejudice*. Every genre is available: Sherlock and Miss Marple, Louis L'Amour westerns, Ray Bradbury science fiction, and Shakespeare and Dickens and Twain and, well, quite enough to go around.

78
From Ducks to Elephants

ASIDE FROM CATS, the two animals whose images are most collected are ducks and elephants. It seems unlikely that even the most intrepid analyst of the psychology and sociology of human beings would like to attempt to explain all this. Some things just are. But it is a given that provides anyone who has such a collector on his on her Christmas list with some easy solutions. There are ducks and elephants to be found in profusion, and at reasonable prices, although there are more inexpensive ducks than elephants, and more *really* expensive ducks than elephants generally available. We're talking about catalogs and gift shops, not museum pieces.

Actually, there is some sense in the price discrepancies. A five-inch wooden duck can be beautiful, but a five-inch elephant doesn't quite convey the majesty of the animal. You can buy quite a spectacular small wooden duck, but a spectacular elephant is likely to be given its proper weight in brass. On the other hand, a full-size duck, a genuine hunter's decoy, is a special class of folk art, and fetches a couple of hundred dollars accordingly, and a great deal more if it is antique.

If you know a collector of either the marshland bird or the jungle giant, your options at under $25 are legion. There is one thing to keep in mind about elephants, however. Some collectors of elephants are superstitious and consider an elephant with a lowered trunk unlucky, unless it is a figure of a mother guiding a calf. Find out if that is the case before you buy.

79
Everywhere Cats!

WHAT IS THE easiest kind of person to find a suitable Christmas present for?

From our experience, it is the cat fanatic. Not everyone who has a cat, or even a couple of cats, is a fanatic, of course, but you will know very quickly when you've met one. Cat fanatics talk about their cats a lot, and anything pertaining to the world of cats will meet with their approval as a present. Every Christmas brings a slew of new cat books, both fiction and nonfiction. Narrative books of either kind, telling the story of a cat or cats that have definite personalities—a book like Cleveland Amory's best-selling *The Cat Who Came for Christmas*—seem a better choice than a care manual. The only problem here is the possibility of duplication—someone else may make a present of the same book, so make sure it is returnable for exchange.

But the cat fanatic will probably appreciate a cat object even more, and they are available in dozens of forms at reasonable prices. There are heavy porcelain doorstops in the shape of cats; planters; papier-mâché cats that are painted with flower patterns; nesting wooden cat boxes; oversize cat magnets; and wooden silhouette cats that are carved so that the tail will dangle over the edge of a windowsill or fireplace. There are also cat calendars, notecards, potholders, tea towels, and even cat jigsaw puzzles and needlepoint kits. You will find cat items in dozens of catalogs, but an especially good source at terrific prices is Lillian Vernon.

80
Ever-Changing Patterns

KALEIDOSCOPES, THOSE ARISTOCRATIC optical toys of the nineteenth century invented by Sir David Brewster in 1815, have had a rather strange history. While some antique kaleidoscopes are worth thousands of dollars, they have gone in and out of favor with the general population several times. There was a period in the 1950s and 1960s when they were virtually unavailable in the United States, although you could readily find them in Italy. These days they are very much back in, featured in many museum and gift catalogs. But most of those are expensive, seldom under $45 and in many cases over $200.

In the last couple of years, however, a number of inexpensive kaleidoscopes have shown up that have a special feature. You can remove the bottom end and change the bits of glass, buttons, colored stones, or whatever at will. Even two or three new pieces of material will provide a different kind of pattern when viewed through the top. If someone you know is a kaleidoscope collector, one of these that you have filled with your own choice of colored bits and pieces will be received with delight. But they are also wonderful presents for children in the seven-to-twelve age bracket, who can amuse themselves endlessly adding and subtracting items to produce new patterns. Kaleidoscopes of this sort, in the under-$25 range (and some sell for half that) are made of simply decorated cardboard and usually come with a few bits in separate envelopes ready to be put in the container end. You will have to keep your eye peeled for these—they have a way of appearing and disappearing from issue to issue of mail-order catalogs. If you see one offered, grab it.

81
A Toy Bonanza

HUMORIST GEORGE PERRET has written, "The more money you spend on a toy, the more likely kids will be to play with the box it came in." This is a great truth. Part of edging toward adulthood is the awareness at about the age of ten that your five-year-old brother or sister or cousin or next-door neighbor's kid of that age has lost total interest in the costly Madame Alexander doll or elaborate build-a-skyscraper set, and is playing with the cheapest stocking present, or yes, even the box the expensive present came in. Of course, there are sophisticated youngsters who are enthralled with the beauty or challenge of the "main" present, but they tend to be exceptions— even the ten-year-old observer may have a sudden realization, "Uh-oh, I remember doing that."

We'll introduce a little a bit of controversy here. If a kid isn't your child or grandchild, you really shouldn't be giving a present that costs over $25 anyway, and if you intend to get anywhere near that amount, avoid the "big stuff" and give the kid a lot of little stuff in one grab-bag of a box.

Chain stores like Walgreens and Wal-Mart are full of inexpensive toys of all kinds, from miniature automobiles to games like jacks, from small animals to miniature vanity sets. Many of these items are under $2, and a box of surprises will give a younger child a lot to get excited about. Miles Kimball would also be a good source for a grab-bag present; the prices are remarkably low and some of the possibilities, like wooden dinosaur kits for assembly, are quite imaginative ($2.98 to $4.49).

Another way to give a child a lot to play with for a modest sum is to select a unified present with a lot of pieces. For example, Hand in Hand (First Step, Ltd.) carries 16-piece miniature kitchen sets for $12.95, as well as two sets of adjustable plastic workshop tools at $12.95 each. The Right Start Catalog also has a number of such items, a standout being 6 wearable plastic helmets, ranging from Grand Prix racer to fire chief, for only $14.95 for all 6. Lots to play with—and easy on the pocketbook.

82
Putting the Pieces Together

Hold on to your hats! You know people who are mad about jigsaw puzzles? Here's how to drive them even crazier. You can take your pick from castles, châteaux, or cathedrals; wizards and dragons; butterflies, fish, birds, and jungle animals; quilts and Fabergé eggs; paintings by everyone from Renoir to Magritte, or make that Degas to Dali; monster submarine sandwiches and shelves of international beers; a whole shopful of baseball momentos or a giant postage stamp collection; and mind-boggling M. C. Escher visual deceptions. . . .

And for the kids, "Animalia" puzzles with hidden words by the stunning Australian artist Graeme Base, or, believe it or not, Barbie in about twenty different costumes.

All of these are from either Bits and Pieces or World Wide Games, and merely begin to suggest the nerve-wracking possibilities available, all for under $20, many only about half that. Of course, jigsaw puzzles also show up in many, many other catalogs, with a special tilt toward the arts or the natural world or old cars or . . . well, you get the idea.

Just for good measure, Bits and Pieces will take your 8-by-10-inch color photograph of your child or yourself or a photo of the old family farm and turn it into a 110-piece jigsaw puzzle for just $16.95. Are they trying to say something about life in general here?

83
A Newlywed Christmas

WHEN THINKING ABOUT Christmas presents for newlyweds, look to the practical. They probably got more than
enough fancy and/or useless presents for their wedding. They
certainly will not need something like a crystal candy dish. But
how about a porcelain enamel three-quart colander in brilliant
red or green? Very Christmassy, and a nice replacement for
the two banged-up old ones they brought to the marriage. These
are $18.50 each from The Wooden Spoon, a company that also
offers something different and very useful, a kiln-fired pot from
Bulgaria that has air holes around the sides. What's it for? To
keep onions in—the circulating air prevents them from sprout-
ing. The handsome covered pot holds three pounds and is
$21.95. This is a present designed to prevent a newlywed spat
over why the onions stored on top of the refrigerator always
seem to end up rolling around the kitchen floor.

With the courtship in the past, the newlyweds are likely
to find themselves eating in more often, even if it is only frozen
food. So how about a kitchen timer, either a bright-green pepper
or a bright-red tomato, $16.50 each from The Paragon? After
all, the newlyweds are still likely to find themselves losing
track of time when they're in one another's company.

Think *practical* and don't be afraid of a little humor.

84
Specialized Soaps

MANY PEOPLE HAVE the notion that a gift of soap is right
up there with socks and underwear in the boring pantheon.
But a lot of others don't look at it that way. Both our mothers
were always delighted to receive fancy soaps that they would
use themselves, or the elegant little packages of miniature guest
soaps to put out when company was coming. You can tell if a
friend is going to appreciate a gift of soap or not just by seeing
what's in that person's bathroom. If there are fresh cakes of
guest soap out when you visit, or even a regular bar of some
fine-milled, exquisitely perfumed soap, you'll know such a gift
would be appreciated. If the soap dish has a used bar of some
supermarket brand in it, forget the whole idea.

Fancy soaps are widely available in department stores and
many pharmacies. Probably the premier soap maker in this
country is Caswell-Massey, whose mail-order catalogs are
among the most elegant and amusing put out by anyone and
will provide you with an hour or so of pleasant entertainment
as well as giving you a lot of gift ideas.

Don't assume that a gift of soap is for women only. Many
men insist upon using only the finest soaps, with masculine
scents like sandalwood. Any man who gardens might particularly appreciate the pumice soap from John Deere, three handsomely wrapped bars in a wooden box ($12.50, or two boxes
for $22.00).

85

Junk Jewelry for Gallivanting

WE CAN'T ALL own—or give—eight-carat diamonds and emeralds the size of a macadamia nut. To judge by the media, most people who do own them wear paste copies most of the time anyway, for fear of being robbed. But it is perfectly possible to assemble a collection of junk jewelry over the years that would do honor to a trunk in Ali Baba's cave. The "top of the line" here is antique junk jewelry—antique means prior to 1940 in this area—and some of the pieces inspired by Art Deco and Art Nouveau but made in the twenties and thirties are quite special. We have several women friends who love this stuff, and have found wonderful examples at flea markets and small antique shops that are so pretty they seem a bargain at under $25.

Contemporary junk jewelry turns up in catalog after catalog, and much of it very nice, too, but the best source we've come across is Nature's Jewelry. They put out a lavishly illustrated eighty-page catalog several times a year. This company cleverly mixes in real silver, turquoise, malachite, and other stones with *faux* counterparts to quite stunning results. The technology of producing faux diamonds, pearls, and semiprecious stones has reached an apex in recent years, and put together in a good design, the end product can be fine indeed. Nature's Jewelry has something for every taste, and excels at cloisonné pieces. They have hundreds of pieces of all kinds of jewelry for under $25.

Another good source of junk jewelry is the Seta Corporation. They sometimes run advertisements that sound too good to be true, but they offer a lot of very good quality and very pretty jewelry, mostly at $19.95. You almost always get a surprise "free gift" as well, and unlike most offers of this kind, the freebies have turned out to be the perfect thing for a twelve-year-old godchild or niece, and sometimes the bonus is superior to just a kid's bauble. A word of warning, however: This is a "contest" company, and once you've ordered something from them, you'll be told you're up for a $10,000 prize about every three weeks. If you can resist this kind of blandishment, the company does provide wide choice and very prompt delivery. A given brochure may contain mostly designs you wouldn't be caught dead in, the next one something you know would be perfect for a certain person. Keep your head and you can do very very well here. What's more, they have a no-questions-asked refund policy, which they do honor.

86
Raising a Special Glass

LIQUOR STORES IN the last two years have been stacked with examples of a new holiday marketing trend: a bottle of vodka, brandy, or liqueur, packed in a decorative box with two glasses, often stamped with the name of the product. This is a cute idea—maybe a little too cute—that can be made much more personal with a modest effort. Pay a visit to one of your local antique shops, the kind that have tables covered with small items for sale. You are likely to find a number of antique glasses, no doubt once part of a complete set of which only two or three remain. This brings their cost down, and there are often some splendid examples for as little as $3 to $5 apiece. Even a matching pair isn't necessary—two different glasses with a red, green, or purple tint can be very beguiling.

You now have $15 or so left with which to purchase a decent bottle of wine or liqueur—but your present will be remembered long after the contents of the bottle have been consumed.

87
Pitchers of All Kinds

NOBODY CAN HAVE too many pitchers, whether they are made of glass, pottery, or good china. A great many are so handsome that they belong out on display. Come party time, a good supply of pitchers can be very helpful in taking care of the wide variety of drink requests, from fruit juices to martinis, that are now so much a part of the social scene. They can also be used to display flowers—dried, fresh, or fake.

In going through the hundreds of catalogs we perused for this book, we discovered something very interesting about pitchers: From the photographs displaying them, it is often extremely difficult to guess what they are going to cost. One pitcher of cobalt-blue glass may be $20, another $90; one imported hand-painted pottery pitcher will be listed at $22, another at $122. That makes pitchers very good presents for people you'd rather not have know you were budget shopping for them.

The variety of pitchers offered changes constantly, but there are a number of sources that can always be counted on to have an enticing array. Williams-Sonoma, Crate & Barrel, the Pottery Barn, and The Wooden Spoon are always a good bet. Although the company does not issue a mail-order catalog, Pier 1 is a terrific place to look if there is a store in your area. The museum catalogs tend to be more highly priced, but Winterthur consistently offers some pitchers that are under $25— last year a particularly handsome one of cobalt glass, for example. A little looking around, and you're sure to find something that is "pitcher perfect."

88
A Christmas Recipe Kit

GOOD FRIENDS WHO are also good cooks regularly exchange recipes with one another. Sometimes it is one that one
person has been served at the other's house, and has requested.
But it can also be a matter of a new discovery offered to a
friend in a spirit of "I just know you'll love this." The exchange
of recipes can be carried a step further by giving a friend not
only a recipe but the main ingredients that are required to
make it. Take, for example, a recipe for a saffron-tinged risotto
with sun-dried tomatoes and olives. One could send the recipe
together with a pound of imported Arborio rice—a must for
first-rate risottos—a package of sun-dried tomatoes, a jar of
first-class olives, and a vial of imported saffron, all individually
wrapped inside a larger box.

The following is a recipe that lends itself wonderfully to
a Christmas Eve dinner, and to this kind of present.

CHRISTMAS FETTUCCINE WITH SALMON CAVIAR
Serves six as a first course, four as a main course

1 pound spinach
  fettuccine
4 tablespoons butter
6 tablespoons cream
1 tablespoon tomato
  paste

¼ teaspoon fine-ground
  pepper
2 tablespoons chopped
  green tops of scallions
2 ounces red salmon
  caviar
salt

Cook the spinach fettuccine according to package
directions. Meantime, in a large nonstick frying pan, melt

123

the butter. Add the cream, the tomato paste, and the pepper (a couple of grindings if not using preground pepper). Cook over medium heat until the cream begins to thicken. Add the chopped green scallion tops. If pasta is not yet done, remove the cream mixture temporarily from the heat. When pasta is just done, turn it off. Return the cream mixture to the heat and stir in the caviar very gently. Taste and add salt if necessary. Strain the fettuccine and fold it into the cream with care. Serve immediately. This dish does not really need parmesan cheese, which changes the delicate flavors, but it can be offered at the table if you wish.

If you were to create a Christmas recipe kit for this dish, send a pound of imported dried fettuccine, a tube of imported tomato paste, and a 2-ounce jar of red salmon caviar along with the recipe.

89
Wool for the Knitter

DO YOU KNOW someone who does a lot of knitting—sweaters, scarves, caps, mittens? Consider giving your friend a surprise boxful of yarn, especially if the knitter is on a fairly tight budget. The raw materials of artneedlework are not cheap and a contribution to the knitter's chestful of wool in many colors will be greatly appreciated.

If you yourself know very little about knitting, be assured that any shop that sells yarn will be able to assist you in putting together a splendid package. It is doubtful that there is any kind of shop in which you will find more helpful personnel, willing to answer with patience and charm any questions you may have.

The same kind of present can be given to a person who does needlepoint—and that number includes many men, notably, actor and former NFL football star Rosey Grier!

90
Gift Certificates for Kids

THERE'S ALWAYS BEEN a good deal of argument about the increasingly common practice of giving gift certificates as Christmas presents. Is this a way of ensuring that the recipient gets exactly what is wanted, or is it the lazy way out? That seems to us to depend on the circumstances. But there's one situation in which a gift certificate is never out of place: as a present for a child between the ages of six and eleven. The child needs to be old enough to understand what's involved, but not too old to have gotten the idea that a $25 gift certificate doesn't amount to much.

Within those age parameters, however, a trip to a store like Toys "Я" Us to pick out a special present or two can be a real treat for a child. The authors are old enough to remember when a crisp new five-dollar bill in a Christmas money envelope could make the heart race with anticipation, and a gift certificate can still have the same effect. Of course, it won't work if the kid is spoiled rotten, but then nothing else will either that doesn't cost an arm and a leg.

91
Games to Learn By

THERE ARE SPLENDID toy stores all across the country, some of them almost legendary institutions, others nearly ubiquitous chains, and if your nerves are in good shape on the appointed day, it can be great fun to have your child take you on a frenetic tear through one of them. That should be part of every child's Christmas memories. But some of the most famous stores seem to have geared their prices to Wall Street raiders and oil barons, while the atmosphere in a mall outlet is hardly conducive to rational thought. This is another area where sitting down in your favorite chair and going through two or three catalogs can be enormously helpful. If the company has a local store, there's no need to incur the added expense of shipping costs, but you will have a better idea of what you want when you go to the store.

This form of homework can be particularly to the point in terms of buying a present in the "games to learn by" category. With the education of American children (or lack of it) a subject of major debate, toy companies have recently been emphasizing games that also teach. These run from the very simple, such as a wooden rectangle that has a child's name cut into it, with letters provided to fit into the cut-out spaces, to quite sophisticated creations that are supposed to teach geography or basic scientific principles. This is an area in which parents will have to make their own judgments about a particular child's interests and learning level. That's all the more reason to look over the possibilities in advance.

92

A Christmas Bon Voyage

Do you know someone who is planning a trip abroad, especially to an area of the world they haven't visited before? Perhaps there is a family that likes to plan a trip with the kids to a different part of the United States every couple of years. Or perhaps there's someone who used to travel a lot but finds it difficult to get around or get away anymore and has to settle for being an armchair traveler. A wonderful place to find a Christmas gift for any of these people is the catalog of The Literate Traveller.

This handsomely produced catalog, replete with line drawings and quotations, offers nearly two-dozen different series of guide books, phrase books covering everything from Finnish to Swahili, and hundreds of individual titles traversing the gamut from humorous memoirs to archaeological overviews. There's something for everyone here, from a *Mystery Reader's Walking Guide* to London or to various smaller cities and towns around the country, to *Our Sisters' London: Feminist Walking Tours*. The snorkler might be fascinated by *Underwater Indonesia;* the animal lover by one of several books on the wildlife of East Africa.

There are books for children as well as adults, and a wide selection of literary classics of the travel genre. What's more, the majority of the books offered are softcover, which means a great many books are under $10, making it possible to put together at least two contrasting volumes. All titles or series are thoroughly covered in what amount to minireviews, so you'll know exactly what you are choosing.

93
Calendar Madness

THE CALENDAR BUSINESS has gone wild in recent years. Every environmental association has one, every museum offers several, there are endless possibilities featuring the cats, dogs, and horses that have always been popular. There are calendars for devotees of every sport from baseball to stock car racing. You can buy a calendar with twelve months of ancient Egyptian masterpieces, or twelve months of Chippendales (we are not talking antique chairs here).

Does this mean that you should forget about the idea of giving anyone a calendar? Not in the least, although that seems to be a trend. Right after last Christmas, we talked to several people who were used to getting at least a couple of elegant calendars every year, but had suddenly received none. They were, of course, desperate. It was almost January and the only ones left in the stores were total rejects that one would feel comfortable hanging only in a closet.

Really nice calendars, from wildlife foundations and museums, are never really going to go out of fashion as gifts. And considering the amount being charged for relatively tacky ones in the average store, the $12 to $18 you can spend for a super calendar featuring eighteenth-century flower prints or photographs by Ansel Adams or Eliot Porter hardly seems extravagant. If you don't give any calendars this year, someone you love isn't going to know what day it is come January 1st, and that would be a pity.

94
A Taste of New England

DOES YOUR CHRISTMAS gift list include anybody who has moved from New England to the Sunbelt? How about someone who loves big weekend breakfasts? Either way, you should acquaint yourself with the catalogs of two Vermont companies, Harrington's and Maple Grove Farms of Vermont. Not if you are on a diet, however; both of these terrific little catalogs tend to induce immediate hunger pangs, if not outright drooling.

While both companies carry smoked hams and turkeys that are considerably beyond our cost limit, they also feature numerous items that are well within the boundaries. Cob-smoked (over corn cobs) bacon and Canadian bacon, Vermont cheeses, maple syrup, pancake mixes, cheesecakes and other bakery products—all are available from both companies. Both have breakfast "sampler" gifts for under $25. Harrington's also carries soups, and Maple Grove Farms has a wide selection of maple candies. Brandied cranberries from Harrington's catches the eye, as does the amusing flask of maple syrup from Maple Grove Farms called "Northern Comfort," which is also available in miniature "nip" bottles. Two packages of the cranberries are $8.45, while the "Northern Comfort" is $12.50 for the flask, $12.95 for six nips.

There is something definitely Christmassy about both these catalogs, starting with their snowy covers.

95
Louisiana Spice

THE CAJUN AND Creole cuisines of Southern Louisiana are perhaps the most distinctive in America. With the assistance of that beaming culinary giant, Paul Prudhomme, the splendors of this deeply flavored cooking have become increasingly popular around the country in recent years. Anyone who likes spicy food would certainly find a gift chosen from the catalogs of Gazin's of New Orleans or Community Kitchens of Baton Rouge a tingling pleasure.

Both catalogs offer foodstuffs, kitchenware, and service dishes. The emphasis at Gazin's is on food. The company has a dazzling array of bottled hot sauces, mustards, preserves, pickles, and dessert toppings. From 1812 Wine Sauce through Melinda's Hot Sauce to Gold Brick sundae sauce, a mixture of milk chocolate and pecans, there are so many tantalizing items it's hard to know what to choose. All kinds of rice mixtures, dried beans, and fancy pastas also beckon. And prices are low enough so that it would be easy to put together a present of three or four different items.

Community Kitchens offers a similar range of products, with a specially good selection of sausages and unusual pastas, including black Calimari Angel Hair and Curry Fettuccine. And there are lots of snazzy cooking and serving pieces at reasonable prices. It almost goes without saying that both companies feature a variety of famous Louisiana coffees and mixes to prepare the deep-fried pastries called beignets that are almost synonymous with midmorning coffee in New Orleans.

96
California Style

OVER THE LAST dozen or so years, California chefs have earned a great reputation for taking the ingredients and dishes of Europe, Asia, and various regions of the United States and giving them a California twist. And because California is one of the great agricultural areas of the world, the state has been in the forefront of the development of American varieties of everything from rice to cheese.

A splendid catalog that concentrates on California-grown products is A Gourmet Taste of Northern California. It features the all-natural jams, dessert toppings, and mustards of Sonoma County's Kozlowski Farms. Sampler packs run from $14.95 for mustards, to $18.95 for raspberry dessert toppings, to a package of 6 jams at $29.95 that could easily be divided into two gifts. Cheeses, olives, pancake mixes, as well as a salsa and blue corn chip package are all available in samplers priced at under $20. Two items of special interest are a selection of calmati, three-grain, and jasmine rices at $13.95, and a 7-ounce box of marzipan fruits and vegetables that are little works of art ($15.95).

California Cuisine is an extremely eclectic catalog full of goodies not only from California but imported from around the world. From the Mendocino white- and dark-chocolate macaroons to the English scone mixes, the bakery choices are especially strong, as is the wide selection of pickled vegetables. Sourdough breads are available, including a $19.95 offer of sourdough rounds to be hollowed out and filled with the contents of the included cans of clam chowder—as you get to the bottom eat the bread, too, Fisherman's Wharf style. Although it specializes in cookware and serving dishes, Williams-Sonoma also has a nice selection of baked goods, candy, sauces, and preserves.

97
Homemade Chutneys

GIFTS OF HOMEMADE jams and jellies are always welcome, but many people are wary of the task of canning foods according to the old-fashioned techniques that allow for shelf storage for many months. An alternative, at least in the case of friends whose homes you will be stopping by during the holiday season, is to make chutneys that need to be refrigerated but will keep nicely for two weeks. A good homemade chutney is unlikely to stay in anyone's refrigerator even that long.

Americans have finally discovered chutneys in all their glory, just as they have salsas. Chutney recipes are turning up all the time in the food magazines and new cookbooks, but here is a personal favorite that has the advantage of a beautiful deep-red Christmas color.

CHRISTMAS CHUTNEY
Makes six cups

6 garlic gloves, peeled and coarsely chopped
1 heaping tablespoon fresh ginger, peeled and chopped
1½ cups red wine vinegar
2 14½-ounce cans peeled whole tomatoes
1½ cups white granu-lated sugar

1 teaspoon salt
¼ teaspoon cayenne pepper
3 tablespoons shelled and coarsely chopped uncolored (green) pistachio nuts

The chopped garlic and ginger need to be reduced to a coarse paste with vinegar in either a blender or a food processor. If a blender is used, add in ½ cup of the vinegar. In a food processor, 1 cup of the vinegar will be necessary because of the broader bottom of the container.

In a porcelain-lined or nonstick pot with a heavy bottom, combine the tomatoes, with their juice, the sugar, and the rest of the vinegar. Bring to a boil and then add the garlic/ginger/vinegar mixture from the blender or food processor bowl as well as the salt and cayenne. Turn the heat down—the chutney should bubble very gently. Cook uncovered, for at least 1½ hours. If too much liquid evap- orates, add water by the quarter cup. The chutney will need to be stirred only about every 20 minutes for the first hour, but then more often as it thickens in the last half hour. The heat should also be further lowered in the last 20 minutes. In the course of cooking the chutney, break up any large pieces of tomato, but there should still be a lot of chunks remaining. When the chutney achieves the consistency of Chinese duck sauce, and coats the back of a spoon, add in the coarsely chopped pistachio nuts and stir for 2 minutes. Remove from the heat, cool, and refrigerate in jars.

This chutney keeps for weeks. Several batches of chutney can be prepared at once, but use separate pots for each recipe.

One friend likes this chutney so much that she mixes it in with plain yogurt, instead of fruit, for a special treat.

In terms of presenting the chutney as a gift, consider buying some special labels. The Personal Touch offers nearly three-inch-square gummed labels in assorted fruit and vegetable designs that leave plenty of room for writing, $12.95 for 100.

98
When Loved Ones Develop Physical Problems

WHEN AN AGING relative or parent begins to develop problems with his sight, hearing, or dexterity, many people have trouble figuring out what kind of present to give. Your mother's failing sight precludes the book on the fine arts you usually give her; a new opera recording won't do since your father's hearing has become so bad; and Aunt Helen's arthritis rules out the needlepoint kits she took such delight in.

Don't fall back on handkerchiefs and ties in order to avoid calling attention to their new problems. Instead, give presents that will help the person go on enjoying life as fully as possible. Large-type editions of books are becoming increasingly available, as are recorded versions of not only classic works but also current best-sellers. The person with impaired sight can still experience the pleasures of a "good read"—and many of the artists who do the reading are front-rank stage actors who can give a whole new meaning to a book. For those with hearing loss, consider facing the problem squarely and giving them videotapes of the great silent movies of the 1920s, especially one of the many collections of comedy short subjects that are now available. And for someone with arthritis of the hands, remember that one of the great frustrations such people face is having terrible difficulty wrapping presents to give to others. Make things easier for them with a collection of various sized designer paper bags, some with Christmas scenes, some with flowers, some with reproductions of paintings, plus some extra-fancy tissue paper. They will then be able to simply slip a gift into one of these handsome bags, tuck tissue paper over the top, and feel no embarrassment at their handiwork.

99
Their Very Own Magazine in the Mail

KIDS LOVE TO get things in the mail, and what could be better than their own magazine subscription? That could be *Sesame Street Magazine* or *Turtle* for children ages two to six; *Child Life, Highlights for Children, Jack and Jill,* or the beautifully illustrated *Cricket* for children in the six-to-ten bracket; or *Disney Adventures* for the eight-to-fourteen-year-old.

To decide which magazine to send as a gift, check out a good newsstand, or the children's section of your local library. A magazine subscription seems an especially appropriate gift from grandparents, godparents, and aunts and uncles, but make sure to clear your selection with the child's mother or father to make sure there's no duplication. The magazines will send a gift announcement card on request, but it seems a nice idea to send the child an actual copy of a previous issue, all wrapped up, so he or she gets to open something and see what's in store over the months ahead.

100
Our Favorite Catalog

OUT OF THE hundreds of catalogs we reviewed in putting together this book, it might well seem difficult to choose just one as our favorite. But in fact, it was not hard at all.

It isn't a large catalog, offering only about 125 gifts. It is issued only once a year, in the autumn. Yet it stands out in many ways. The catalog is that of the Christian Children's Fund Craft Cooperative. You may have seen National Chairperson Sally Struthers talking about this organization on television. Founded fifty-four years ago, CCF is a nonsectarian humanitarian organization that works in thirty-six countries around the world, including the United States. It raises nearly one hundred million dollars a year, 80 percent of which goes to children and their families across the globe. Within each country only nationals are employed as field and program administrators. But please don't get us wrong, this is not our favorite catalog because of the good work done by the CCF. It is our favorite catalog because it offers objects of great beauty at modest prices; but put the emphasis on the beauty.

Nothing either of us has ever bought from CCF has failed to be even more striking than it looked in the color catalog. Each object is handmade, and so, no two are quite alike, but all are of extraordinary quality. Whether it has been a lacquered hand-carved wooden duck box from Thailand, a reed flute from Bolivia, a mask from Indonesia, or a necklace from India, we have always found ourselves saying, "Oh, how wonderful." In fact, a number of objects that were intended as gifts somehow never got wrapped up and sent off until we started ordering duplicates.

The great majority of the crafts in the CCF catalog are under $25, and many are half or a third that. Everything we have ordered has arrived very quickly, well-packed, and in perfect shape, but CCF will not only refund your money if you aren't satisfied but also pay the postage. It is hard to imagine anyone being dissatisfied with these wonderful objects, however. That people living in such poverty can produce such beauty gives a lift to the Christmas spirit.

101
Small Things in Big Packages

ALTHOUGH THE AUTHORS grew up at opposite ends of the country and almost a decade apart, our families had a lot of very similar ideas about Christmas. One present from a relative could be opened on Christmas Eve, our choice, but that was it until the next day. On Christmas morning, each member of the family opened one present at a time while everyone else watched to see what the surprise would be. That was even true for our stockings. We both remember young friends calling up and saying, "You haven't finished yet? We got through hours ago!" They came from families in which everything was opened simultaneously in a wild fifteen-minute melee. We thought it was a lot more fun the way we did it.

Both our familes also went in for deceptive packaging in a big way. Everyone in the family always got something that was quite small but had been put into a very big box that was wrapped to the nines. Sometimes the small present inside was something particularly nice; sometimes it was something silly— or even those ubiquitous socks. On the other hand, there were years when somebody's "main" present—a very-first wrist-watch, for example—would be lodged in the toe of the stocking. Every Christmas for nearly twenty years, one of our mothers' stockings always contained a miniature bottle of bourbon that had first shown up there when the miniatures first appeared in the early 1950s. It spent all year on her bureau and mysteriously disappeared each Christmas Eve.

Christmas is not about costly gifts. It is about family traditions, surprises, and jokes. It is about raising children who can look back forty years later and say, "Such good times." We hope that some of the suggestions we have made in this book will help to make your Christmases more fun than ever, without breaking the bank.

Merry Christmas to all!

A Note About the List of Catalogs

All of the catalogs listed on the following pages accept major credit cards unless otherwise noted. There are only a couple of firms that prefer personal checks or money orders. A few companies do not take phone orders, for the simple reason that they handle so many small items that it would not be economical to deal with anything other than a mail order. You will discover that there are a few companies for which no street address is given. This is not an error. There do remain a number of companies whose presence in a town or small city is so central to that locale that no street address is required.

List of Catalogs

Abracadabra Fun and Magic
P.O. Box 712
Dept. C-570
Middlesex, NJ 08846-0712
1-908-805-0200

Almond Plaza
P.O. Box 75
Maumee, OH 43537-0075
1-800-225-6887

Art and Artifact
A Barnes & Noble
Catalogue
126 Fifth Avenue
New York, NY 10011
1-800-344-2470

The Art Institute of Chicago
Michigan Avenue at Adams
Street
Chicago, Il 60603
1-708-299-5470

Back to Basics Toys
8802 Monard Drive
Silver Spring, MD 20910
1-800-356-5360

Barnes & Noble
126 Fifth Avenue
New York, NY 10011
1-800-242-6675

Berea College Crafts
CPO 2347
Berea, KY 40404
1-800-347-3892

Bits and Pieces
1 Puzzle Place—B80166
Stevens Point, WI 54481-7199
1-715-341-3521

Brooks Stamp Co.
P.O. Box 62
Brooklyn, NY 11229
1-718-763-6843

Brookstone
Hard-To-Find Tools
5 Vose Farm Road
Peterborough, NH 03458
1-800-926-7000

143

Burpee Seed Co.
300 Park Avenue
Warminster, PA 18974
1-215-674-4900

California Cuisine
3501 Taylor Drive
Ukaih, CA 95482
1-800-753-8558

Casual Living
5401 Hangar Court
P.O. Box 31273
Tampa, FL 33631-3273
1-800-843-1881

Caswell-Massey Co., Ltd.
100 Enterprise Place
Dover, DE 19901
1-800-366-0500

Char-Broil
P.O. Box 1300
Columbia, GA 31993-2499
1-800-241-8981

The Chef's Catalog
3215 Commercial Avenue
Northbrook, IL 60062-1900
1-800-338-3232

Childcraft (Toys that Teach)
Childcraft, Inc.
P.O. Box 29149
Mission, KS 66201-9149
1-800-631-5657

Christian Children's Fund
2821 Emerywood Parkway
Richmond, VA 23261-5066
1-800-366-5896

Classics in the Making
Mason & Sullivan
586 Higgins Crowell Road
West Yarmouth
Cape Cod, MA 02673
1-800-933-3010

Community Kitchens
P.O. Box 2311, Dept. HN
Baton Rouge, LA 70821-2331
1-800-832-0572

Condé Nast's Portfolio
P.O. Box 8002, Dept 568
Hillard, OH 43062-8002
1-800-323-5265

Constructive Playthings
1227 East 119th Street
Grandview, MO 64030-1117
1-800-832-0572

Crate & Barrel
P.O. Box 9059
Wheeling, IL 60090-9059
1-800-323-5461

Daedalus Books
P.O. Box 9132
Hyattsville, MD 20781-0932
1-800-395-2665

Dick Blick
P.O. Box 1267
Galesburg, IL 61401
1-800-447-8192

Dover Publications, Inc.
31 East 2nd Street
Mineola, NY 11501
1-516-294-7000

Duncraft
Penacook, NH 03303-9020
1-603-224-0200

Edmund Scientific Co.
101 East Gloucester Pike
Barrington, NJ 08007-1380
1-609-547-8880

Enterprise Art
P.O. Box 2918
Largo, FL 34649
No Phone Orders

Ethel M. Chocolates
P.O. Box 98505
Las Vegas, NV 89193-8505
1-800-438-4356

Exposures
2800 Hoover Road
Stevens Point, WI 54481
1-800-222-4947

The Farmer's Daughter
P.O. Box 1071
Nags Head, NC 27959
1-800-423-2196

Flax Art & Design
1699 Market Street
P.O. Box 7216
San Francisco, CA 94120-7216
1-800-547-7778

Fleetwood
(First Day Covers)
One Unicorn Center
Cheyenne, WY 82008
1-307-634-5911

The Fun House
Box 1225
Newark, NJ 07101
No Phone Orders

Gardener's Eden
P.O. Box 7307
San Francisco, CA 94120-7307
1-415-421-4242

Gazin's
2910 Toulouse Street
P.O. Box 19221
New Orleans, LA 70179-0221
1-504-482-0302

G. B. Ratto & Company
International Grocers, Inc.
821 Washington Street
Oakland, CA 94607
1-800-228-3515

Godiva
P.O. Box 4339
Reading, PA 19606
1-800-447-9393

A Gourmet Taste Of
Northern California
428 Mendocino Avenue
P.O. Box 2768
Santa Rosa, CA 95405
1-800-538-2783

Graphik Dimensions Ltd.
41-23 Haight Street
Flushing, NY 11355-4247
1-800-221-0262

Hand in Hand
(First Step, Ltd.)
550 Lisbon Street
P.O. Box 821
Lewiston, ME 04240
1-800-639-1150

Hank Lee's Magic Factory
24 Lincoln Street
Boston, MA 02111
1-617-482-8749

Harriet Carter
Dept. 31
North Wales, PA 19455
1-215-361-5151

Harrington's
Main Street
Richmond, VT 05477
1-802-434-4444

Harry and David
P.O. Box 712
Medford, OR 97501
1-800-547-3033

HearthSong
P.O. Box B
Sebastapol, CA 95473-0601
1-800-325-2502

H. E. Harris & Co.
P.O. Box 7082
Portsmouth, NH 03802-7082
1-603-433-0400

Herrington
3 Symmes Drive
Londonderry, NH 03053
1-603-437-4638

Highlights for Children
2300 West Fifth Avenue
P.O. Box 269
Columbus, OH 43216-0269
No Phone Orders

Hold Everything
P.O. Box 800
Concord, MA 01742-0005
1-800-262-8600

Home Decorator's Collection
2025 Concourse Drive
St. Louis, MO 63146-4178
1-800-245-2217

Initials
P.O. Box 246
Elmira, NY 14902
1-800-444-8758

Into the Wind Kite Catalog
1408 Pearl Street
Boulder, CO 80302
1-303-449-5356

John Deere
1400 Third Avenue
Moline, IL 61265
1-800-544-2122

Just For Kids
75 Paterson Street
P.O. Box 15006
New Brunswick, NJ 08906-5006
1-800-654-6963

Karl Bissinger French Confections
The Chocolate Catalogue
3983 Gratiot Street
St. Louis, MO 63110
1-800-325-8881

King Arthur Flour
The Baker's Catalogue
R.R. 2 Box 56
Norwich, VT 05055
1-800-827-6836

Land's End for Kids
Land's End, Inc.
1 Land's End Lane
Dodgeville, WI 53595
1-800-356-4444

Learn and Play (Troll)
100 Corporate Drive
Mahwah, NJ 07430
1-800-247-6106

Levenger's
975 South Congress Avenue
Delray Beach, FL 33445-4628
1-800-544-0880

Lillian Vernon
Virginia Beach, VA 23479-0002
1-914-633-6300

Lilly's Kids
Lillian Vernon Corporation
Virginia Beach, VA 23479-0002
1-914-633-6300

The Literate Traveller
8306 Wilshire Boulevard
Suite 591
Beverly Hills, CA 90211
1-310-398-8781

Maple Grove Farms of Vermont
167 Portland Street
St. Johnsburg, VT 05819
1-802-748-3136

Mauna Loa Macadamia Nut Corp.
Mainland Expediting Center
6523 North Galena Road
P.O. Box 1771
Peoria, IL 61656
1-800-832-9993

The Metropolitan Museum
of Art
P.O. Box 255 Gracie Station
New York, NY 10028
1-800-468-7386

Miles Kimball
41 West Eighth Avenue
Oshkosh, WI 54906
No phone orders or credit
cards

The Mind's Eye
P.O. Box 1060
Petaluma, CA 94953
1-800-227-2020

Museum of Fine Arts,
Boston
Catalog Sales Dept.
P.O. Box 1044
Boston, MA 02120-0900
1-800-225-5592

The Museum of Modern Art
Mail Order Department
11 West 53 Street
New York, NY 10019-5401
1-800-447-MOMA

Music for Little People
Box 1460
Redway, CA 95560
1-800-346-4445

The Music Stand
1 Rockdale Plaza
Lebanon, NH 03766
1-802-295-7944

Mystic Stamp Company
24 Mill Street
Camden, NY 13316
1-315-245-2690

National Wildlife Federation
1400 16th Street, N.W.
Washington, DC 20036-
2266
1-800-432-6564

The Nature Company
P.O. Box 188
Florence, KY 41022
1-800-227-1114

Nature's Jewelry
27 Industrial Avenue
Chelmsford, MA 01824-
3692
1-800-333-3235

Northstyle
North Word Press, Inc.
P.O. Box 1360
Minocqua, WI 54548
1-800-336-5666

One Step Ahead
P.O. Box 46
Deerfield, IL 60015
1-800-344-7550

Oxfam America
P.O. Box 831
Lewiston, ME 04240
1-800-639-2141

The Paragon
89 Tom Harvey Road
Westerly, RI 02891
1-800-343-3095

Park Seed
P.O. Box 31
Greenwood, SC 29648-0031
1-803-223-7333

Past Times
280 Summer Street
Boston, MA 02210-1182
1-800-621-6020

Pepperidge Farm
Mail Order Company, Inc.
P.O. Box 119
Route 145
Clinton, CT 06413
1-800-243-9314

The Personal Touch
P.O. Box 1623
Elmira, NY 14902
1-607-733-6313

Plow & Hearth
301 Madison Road
P.O. Box 830
Orange, VA 22960-0492
1-800-627-1712

The Pottery Barn
Mail Order Dept.
P.O. Box 7044
San Francisco, CA 94120-7044
1-800-922-5507

Promises Kept, Inc.
2525 Xenium Lane
P.O. Box 47368
Plymouth MN 55447
1-800-888-3545

REI (Recreational
Equipment, Inc.)
P.O. Box 88125
Seattle, WA 98138-2125
1-800-426-4840

Rent Mother Nature
52 New Street
P.O. Box 193
Cambridge, MA 02238
1-617-354-5430

The Right Start Catalog
Right Start Plaza
5334 Sterling Center Drive
Westlake Village, CA 91361
1-800-548-8531

Script City
8033 Sunset Boulevard—
Suite 1500
Hollywood, CA 90046
1-213-871-0707

See's Candies
210 El Camino Real
South San Francisco, CA
94080
1-800-347-7337

Seta Corporation
6400 East Rogers Circle
Boca Raton, FL 33499
1-407-994-2211

Shepherd's Garden Seeds
30 Irene Street
Torrington, CT 06790
1-203-482-3638

Signals
WGBH Educational
Foundation
1000 Westgate Drive
St. Paul, MN 55114
1-800-669-5225

The Smart Toys Catalog
23880 Commerce Park Drive
Beachwood, OH 44122
1-800-238-8697

Smith and Hawken
25 Corte Madera
Mill Valley, CA 94941
1-415-383-2000

Smithsonian Institution
Dept. 0006
Washington, DC 20073-0006
1-800-322-0344

Southwest Indian
Foundation
P.O. Box 86
Gallup, NM 87302-0001
1-505-863-4037

The Squire's Choice
Suite 110
2000 West Cabot Boulevard
Langhorne, PA 19047
1-800-523-6163

Sundance
Customer Service Center
1909 South, 4250 West
Salt Lake City, UT 84104
1-800-422-2770

Sunnyland Farms, Inc.
Albany, GA 31706-8200
1-912-883-3085

Swiss Colony
1112 7th Avenue
Monroe, WI 53566
1-608-328-8812

Treasures from Your
National Parks
America's National Parks
1100 East Hector Street
Suite 105
Conshohocken, PA 19428
1-800-821-2903

Toys to Grow On
P.O. Box 17
Long Beach, CA 90801
1-800-874-4242

UNICEF
1 Children's Boulevard
P.O. Box 182233
Chattanooga, TN 37422
1-800-553-1200

Voice of the Mountains
The Vermont Country Store
P.O. Box 3000
Manchester Center, VT
05255-3000
1-802-362-2400

Whale Gifts
Center for Marine
Conservation
1725 DeSales Street
Washington, DC 20036
1-800-227-1929

What On Earth
2451 Enterprise East
Parkway
Twinsburg, OH 44087
1-216-963-6555

White Flower Farm
Litchfield, CT 06759-0050
1-800-888-7756

Williams-Sonoma
Mail Order Dept.
P.O. Box 7456
San Francisco, CA 94120-7456
1-800-541-2233

Winterthur Museum and
Gardens
Winterthur, DE 19735
1-800-767-0500

Wireless
Minnesota Public Radio
1000 Westgate Drive
St. Paul, MN 55114
1-800-669-9999

The Wisconsin Cheeseman
P.O. Box 1
Madison, WI 53701
1-608-258-3000

Wolferman's
One Muffin Lane
P.O. Box 15913
Lenexa, KS 66215-5913
1-800-999-0619

The Wooden Spoon
Route 145, Heritage Park
P.O. Box 931
Clinton, CT 06413-0931
1-800-431-2270

World Wide Games
P.O. Box 517
Colchester, CT 06415-0571
1-800-243-9232

World Wildlife Fund
Catalog
P.O. Box 224
Peru, IN 46970
1-800-833-1600

The Write Touch Catalog
Rytex Company
5850 West 80th Street
Dept. K912
P.O. Box 68188
Indianapolis, IN 46268-0188
1-800-288-6824

Index